D1785480

The POWER of Hope

The POWER of Hope

*Discovering the Secrets, Keys
and Promises of the Kingdom*

By Ricki Pepin
In Collaboration with
Pastors Danny & Cheri Miller

XULON PRESS

Xulon Press
2301 Lucien Way #415
Maitland, FL 32751
407.339.4217
www.xulonpress.com

© 2021 by Ricki Pepin
in Collaboration with Pastors Danny & Cheri Miller

All rights reserved solely by the author. The author guarantees all contents are original and do not infringe upon the legal rights of any other person or work. No part of this book may be reproduced in any form without the permission of the author.

Due to the changing nature of the Internet, if there are any web addresses, links, or URLs included in this manuscript, these may have been altered and may no longer be accessible. The views and opinions shared in this book belong solely to the author and do not necessarily reflect those of the publisher. The publisher therefore disclaims responsibility for the views or opinions expressed within the work.

Unless otherwise indicated, Scripture quotations taken from the King James Version (KJV) – *public domain.*

Scripture quotations taken from the New King James Version (NKJV). Copyright © 1982 by Thomas Nelson, Inc. Used by permission. All rights reserved.

Scripture quotations taken from the New American Standard Bible (NASB). Copyright © 1960, 1962, 1963, 1968, 1971, 1972, 1973, 1975, 1977, 1995 by The Lockman Foundation. Used by permission. All rights reserved.

Scripture quotations taken from the New Century Version (NCV). Copyright © 2005 by Thomas Nelson, Inc. Used by permission. All rights reserved.

Paperback ISBN-13: 978-1-66282-664-1
Ebook ISBN-13: 978-1-66282-665-8

PREFACE

You've probably heard the saying, "The best laid plans of mice and men oft times go astray." So it is with this book. Originally titled, "The Apocalypse! Unveiling the End Times," it has now been re-titled, "The POWER of Hope."

The theme of this book is all about a hope and a future. It is positive. It is encouraging. It is life-changing if you study the verses set out and apply them personally. The former title was meant to convey this "revelation" (the true meaning of the word "apocalypse"). When we are walking through "end times" we are rapidly approaching the hope and excitement of "new times." Unfortunately, that was not the message the original title was conveying and people shied away from what sounded dark and depressing.

So, we have a new cover and a new title to better attract people with a message we all need: "The POWER of Hope." Take your time to ponder the secrets, keys and promises revealed on its pages. You will be blessed and empowered as you discover what it means to be a "son of God" and your exciting and fulfilling role in the kingdom of God! Get ready! Your adventure is about to begin!

DEDICATION

This research and book are dedicated to Jesus Christ, the Son of the living God. It is further dedicated to the sons of God who are following in His footsteps: May you discover your true identity in Christ, find other sons, and walk out your victorious and God-ordained destinies in this world.

ACKNOWLEDGMENTS

This book would never have been started without the teaching, leading and inspiration of Pastors Danny & Cheri Miller in their dedicated and committed church, Wings of Love Crusades, in Springfield, Ohio. Their insights and patient week-by-week instruction and discussions opened an entirely new avenue of study of God's Word. Their use of primary source historical texts, alongside scripture, provided a deeper understanding of the Bible and the times in which Jesus lived.

Further personal investigation with the use of the Principle Approach to education – biblical principles, definitions, leading questions, more primary source documents – brought even more clarity in some places, and yet more questions in others. This method of education was used by our Founding Fathers to research, reason, relate and record the truth in any subject. It works. I used it when I homeschooled my children and the results were profound in teaching them how to become deep thinkers.

This book could never have been finished without my two wonderful editors/critics: My beloved other half – Michael Pepin – an engineer with multiple technical degrees, who also has a great eye for detail and precision in written documents; and Tabitha Miller, English Faculty member and PhD candidate at Pitt Community college, who possesses the rare talents of detailed editorial scrutiny along with critical reasoning skills. Thank you both so much!

You are all true sons of God, using your talents for His glory. May you each be abundantly blessed for your contributions of time and expertise in the completion of this book.

TABLE OF CONTENTS

CHAPTER ONE

PROLOGUE
A PERSONAL LETTER TO THE READER –
YOUR ADVENTURE BEGINS!

Dear Reader,

Apocalypse. End Times. Hope. Kingdom of God. These words evoke thoughts that make your heart beat a little faster and your mind spin into hyper drive. What do they mean? Are these terms related? What is about to happen? How will it affect you and your loved ones?

You are about to embark on what could be the most important adventure of your life – your own personal study of these themes. Many books have been written and sermons preached on these topics, yet there is still much confusion and disagreement within the body of believers. This book is designed for you to take responsibility and ownership of what you believe through the use of *primary source* study tools – original historical writings.

Our Founding Fathers used a method of education known as the Principle Approach. Rather than relying on the teaching of others, this system enables students to begin to think and reason for themselves from a biblical foundation. Instead of being told *what* to think, the Principle Approach uses primary source documents, definitions from Noah Webster's 1828 Dictionary, seven biblical principles and leading questions to help students learn *how* to find truth and think for themselves.

You will be taught how to use the Four R's: Research – Reason – Relate – Record. In so doing you will begin to discover truth as it is disclosed to you personally by God's Holy Spirit and will not have to depend on "second-hand" revelation. In addition, your main "tools" will be *primary source* materials like <u>Strong's Concordance</u>, <u>American Dictionary of the English Language</u> (also known as <u>Webster's 1828</u>).

Using primary source volumes is of paramount importance as they are first-hand reports. Today, there are revisionist historical accounts *and* revisionist dictionaries in wide use. If these historical revisions simply include primary source stories that were previously omitted, then they are bringing forth more truth. However, most revisionists are seeking to re-write history to promote their way of thinking, ignoring the truth. We must learn to discern which is which.

On the other hand, rewriting definitions is an attempt to alter an absolute. Words mean what they mean and their definitions do not change. They are not subject to interpretation. They do not evolve. Our usage of them may change, but our mis-application does not alter their original meaning. Founding Father Noah Webster was a master of 27 languages so we can rely on the accuracy of his definitions as a source of original usage and truth.

For example, we are being bombarded today by people speaking of the end times using the word apocalypse. This is a correct translation of the Greek word - *apokalupsis* - used in the New Testament for *revelation*. My computer Thesaurus gives synonyms such as these:

- apocalypse - *disaster, catastrophe, Judgment Day, end of the world, destruction*

This is very interesting in light of the fact that the word revelation (Greek *apokalupsis*) is defined by <u>Strong's Concordance</u> and <u>Webster's 1828 Dictionary</u>, both primary sources that have not been altered by revisionism, very differently:

- revelation *(#602 – apokalupsis) – disclosure: appearing, coming, manifestation, be revealed, revelation* (<u>Strong's Concordance</u>)
- apocalypse – *revelation; discovery; disclosure. The name of a book of the New Testament containing many discoveries or predictions written by St. John.* (<u>Webster's 1828</u>)

Briefly using the Four R's, let's look at what we just found:

- Research – We discovered the true definition of apocalypse.
- Reason – It is very different from revisionist definitions - simply the revealing of something yet to be discovered.
- Relate – It is not inherently disastrous as we have been taught and could even include good news.
- Record – Write down this new understanding in a journal for later applications in other questions that

will be searched out as we look for truth about the end times.

And how does hope and the Kingdom of God tie into the end times? End times evokes fear and apprehension. Hope evokes an expectation for something far better. This is why we re-titled this book, <u>The POWER of Hope – Discovering the Secrets, Keys and Promises of the Kingdom.</u> We are seeking to help the reader discover the truth and the power and peace that lie within it. It is not enough to simply *believe* a thing. We must truly *know* it. We must not believe just because we have been taught by others. We must study deeply for ourselves.

Our greatest desire for the reader is that you will read this book carefully, prayerfully and *study for yourself* to unveil the truth. Search it out. Don't depend on what someone else has told you: *"Be diligent to <u>present your-self</u> approved to God, a worker who does not need to be ashamed, rightly dividing the word of truth"* (2 Timothy 2:15, NKJV). You will probably not agree with all that is written in these pages, and that is fine because our hope is not to sway you to our point of view. We, the authors, are also *works in progress* and make no claims to have all the answers.

Our hope is that you'll rise to the challenge of learning straight from the Holy Spirit and in doing so will strengthen your relationship with your Creator as you gain revelation knowledge. We may indeed be entering the last days, but as you will read in these pages, we do not believe this is the end, but rather a new beginning. Find your role as this reality unfolds. For God has created you as a unique individual with an incredibly important and distinct purpose on this earth, here and now. As you find your purpose, you will find your life.

We must be working at getting closer to God, hearing from Him directly, in these challenging and sometimes perilous days. Your path may change as the world changes, but as long as Jesus is your guide you do not need to worry. Put on your spiritual thinking cap. The most exciting journey of your life is about to begin.

In His service and for His glory –

Ricki Pepin
Pastors Danny & Cheri Miller

CHAPTER TWO

THE KINGDOM

"Many there are who would stay in the tranquil Valley of Ignorance. [But those who desire to learn truth and persevere] will find beyond the icy peaks of struggle lies the peace and beauty of the Infinite Garden of Knowledge." – The Dead Sea Scrolls

OUR DILEMMA

"I can't go with you to church this morning," my preacher husband declared with both frustration and conviction. "I can't preach another sermon until I find out the truth."

After ministering for over 20 years, we were about to embark on a new journey – a search for truth about the end times message. It would not prove to be an easy or short trip. There was a mountain of learning looming before us, and we had so many questions about scriptures that did not seem to match what we had been taught.

We grew up believing that the world was coming to an end in our lifetime. The preaching of the day reminded us at every turn: "Don't polish brass on a sinking ship." "Why care about this world when we are all going to fly away?" The ministries all preached it; the music sang about it, and all everyone talked about was getting out of this world. Any bad news - weather disasters, political unrest, family disintegration - was attributed to "signs of the end times."

But something in our spirit would not stop asking, "Is that what this is really all about?" Exactly what were the prophets referring to when they spoke of the "last days" and the "end of the world?" What did Jesus teach about these times? Just what (and where!) is the kingdom of heaven? And what is our part, as believers, in all of it?

We invite you to put on your spiritual thinking cap and pull on your hiking boots and join in on this trek for truth.

WHERE IS THE KINGDOM OF HEAVEN?

Jesus was a master teacher, so checking out his words about the kingdom of God, also referred to as the kingdom of heaven, seems like a great place to begin our investigation.

In answer to his disciples' query about prayer, Jesus instructs them to pray by saying, in part, "...*Your kingdom come, Your will be done <u>on earth</u> as it is in heaven...*" (Matthew 6:10, NASB). Jesus tells His disciples to pray that God's kingdom should come [on earth] so that His will could be done *on earth* the same way it is done in heaven.

Could this mean that the kingdom of heaven could be on earth?...that I don't have to die to get there? Let's look further.

The Pharisees question Jesus specifically about the kingdom of God: *"Now when He was asked by the Pharisees when the kingdom of God would come, He answered them and said, 'The kingdom of God does not come with observation; nor will they say, 'See here!' or 'See there!' For indeed, the kingdom of God is within you"* (Luke 17:20-21, NKJV).

If something is within me, inside me, as this scripture says, and my body is here on this earth, then that which is *in* me is necessarily also located *on* this earth. So, if the kingdom of God is within me, then the kingdom of God must be *on this earth,* not a place I'll go to someday after death.

WHAT IS THE KINGDOM OF HEAVEN?

Noah Webster, master of 27 languages and author of the original <u>American Dictionary of the English Language</u>, defines kingdom as – *the territory subject to a king.*

What part of ourselves do we subject to Jesus' authority when we are born again? Does salvation not begin in our mind and heart? *"...believe in your heart [that Jesus is Lord and]... you will be saved* (Romans 10:9, NASB).

We must choose to subject our thoughts to His kingship, His kingdom. Therefore, the kingdom of God is in the human heart and mind that has deliberately chosen to enter this domain. And what a great choice: *"For the Kingdom of God is...righteousness, peace and joy..."* (Romans 14:17, NKJV)

Peace and joy are internal thoughts and attitudes. Therefore, to be in God's kingdom does *not* refer to a physical, geographical location. Rather, living in God's kingdom means mentally submitting to the rule, reign and authority of God on a daily basis.

However, these *internal* thoughts will translate into *external* actions: *"For as he thinks in his heart, so is he...* (Proverbs 23:7 NKJV) Living in the kingdom of God will be visible in this world as we practice actions that habitually reflect the will and teachings of Christ daily, in our homes, on the job, in the community, as husbands, wives, parents, friends, citizens, etc. Could this dual manifestation - earth and heaven, flesh and spirit - be what Jesus meant when He prayed, *"Your kingdom come. Your will be done in earth, as it is in heaven"* (Matthew 6:10, NKJV)?

Living in the kingdom of God/heaven means we are in agreement, in covenant, with God and His established order, in thought, word and deed – in spirit and in flesh. The connection between covenant and kingdom is vital to our understanding and recognizing the nature and timing of the kingdom of Heaven in the old and new covenant.

WHEN WAS/IS/WILL BE THE KINGDOM OF HEAVEN?

The kingdom of God has always existed because God has always existed. Our first introduction to it can be seen in the Old Testament. God chose to demonstrate to the whole world the value of living under His rule, reign and authority by entering into a covenant with Abraham's descendants, the Israelites. When Israel was obedient to God's rule, reign and authority they found power, peace and rich meaning in life. When they departed from God's rule, reign and authority they suffered heartaches, setbacks and adversity. Why? Because when we disconnect from God and the life He calls us to live, we get inferior results. All "living" bears fruit. Living with God bears one kind of fruit. Living without God cannot possibly bear the same fruit, any more than an apple tree can produce oranges.

The Jewish old covenant (Old Testament) and kingdom were temporary prototypes that would be replaced by the Messiah's eternal kingdom (new covenant/New Testament). How do we know this? Because Daniel prophesies about it: *"And in the days of these kings shall the God of heaven set up a kingdom which shall never be destroyed...and it shall stand forever"* (Daniel 2:44, NKJV). How long would this kingdom last? Daniel says forever; it will never be destroyed.

But when would this kingdom be established? Daniel says, "in the days of these kings." What kings? Scholars agree that the four earthly kingdoms Daniel describes in Chapter 2 and 7 are one and the same. They began in Daniel's day and successively unfolded, one immediately after the other, and were Babylon, Medo-Persia, Greece and the old Roman Empire, respectively.

Daniel records that during – not after – the time of the fourth kingdom (the old Roman Empire) one like the Son of Man (the Messiah) was to come on the clouds and establish his everlasting kingdom (Daniel 7:13-14, NKJV). This would happen "in the times [days] of those kings" (Daniel 2:44, NKJV).

What major event in history happened at this time in history that Daniel is speaking about? The birth of Christ, the King of the new eternal kingdom!

Does the New Testament corroborate the timing of this new kingdom's arrival? What does John the Baptist preach about the coming kingdom? *"Repent, for the kingdom of heaven is at hand"* (Matthew 3:2, NASB). To repent is to change your heart and mind. Something that is "at hand" is close enough to reach out and touch. His message to the people of *his day* who came to hear him was meant to change *their* thinking and hearts because the kingdom was coming *soon.*

What about Jesus? What did He say about the arrival of the kingdom? *"From that time [when Jesus heard that John had been put in prison] Jesus began to preach and to say, 'Repent, for the kingdom of heaven is at hand'"* (Matthew 4:17, NKJV). His message is identical to that of John the Baptist.

In Luke 21:5-6 Jesus speaks to His disciples about the temple and its imminent destruction. Historically, we know this occurred in 70 A.D. This destruction of the Jewish temple was to bring the <u>end</u> to the prototype Old Testament covenant of animal sacrifices, and forever establish the New Testament covenant of Christ's shed blood and redemption of all mankind. Notice that Jesus ties this event even more emphatically to the *nearness* of the kingdom of God: *"...when you see these things come to pass, know that the kingdom of God is <u>near at hand</u>"* (Luke 22:31, NKJV).

After the death and resurrection of Christ, when Paul writes to the Colossians, he tells Christians that God *"rescued us from the domain of darkness and transferred us to the kingdom of His beloved son"* (Colossians 1:13, NASB). Paul used the past tense! The kingdom had come and those living and reading his letter were already in it! It was a done deal! (See also Romans 10:15-18 that speaks, in past tense, to the fact that this gospel of the new kingdom and covenant *"went into all the earth, and their words to the ends of the world."*)

How do I get into the kingdom? Recognize and acknowledge in your mind, heart and spirit that Jesus Christ, son of the living God, is King, and surrender your will to His. *"For God so loved the world, that He gave His only begotten Son, that whosoever believes in Him should not perish, but have everlasting life."* (John 3:16 NKJV)

IN SUMMARY - HISTORICALLY

From Pentecost in 33 A.D. to the fall of the Jewish temple system, God was building a new kingdom. It was a work in progress, told about in Acts and the epistles. Paul details this *transition* of the old testament/covenant to the new testament/covenant clearly in 2 Corinthians 3:4-18, referring to it as the veil that has been removed, taken away, so that we can now see with an open face.

The final sign that the new, eternal kingdom (promised in Daniel 2:44) was complete was the fall of the temple in Jerusalem (Luke 21:31), which occurred in 70 A.D. No more temple building. No more animal sacrifices. No more Old Covenant. The new temple is the body of the believer (1 Corinthians 3:16). The only sacrifice needed was Jesus, and that was finished. This is the New Covenant and the consummation of the new, eternal kingdom.

A voice from heaven declares the entrance and significance of this new kingdom on earth – *"The kingdom of the <u>world</u> has become the kingdom of our Lord and of His Christ; and He will reign forever and ever"* (Revelation 11:15, NASB).

BUT WHAT ABOUT TODAY?

If the kingdom of heaven is here now, there are some serious questions that need to be addressed:

If we are in the kingdom now, why is there pain and suffering in this world? Why do we think there should be no pain in the kingdom? Is God in the Kingdom of Heaven? Of course, He is. Do you think He experiences pain in his mind and heart as He watches events unfold here on earth? How could He not? The kingdom is not a place of euphoria. *"...and God shall wipe away all tears from their eyes."* (Revelation 7:17, NKJV) The promise is to comfort us in our pain, to wipe away the tears, not that there won't be any. In addition, pain can be your best friend in this life as a warning sign that you need to attend to a physical problem or illness.

If we are in the kingdom now, why does secularism reign? The <u>Tormont Webster's Illustrated Encyclopedic Dictionary</u> defines secularism as – *The view that religious considerations should be excluded from civil affairs or public education.* Many Christians share this view which is why we find ourselves in our current situation in finances, government, schools. However, secularism is a complete lack of understanding that God is God over all people, things and institutions – no exceptions. When the church gives up its responsibilities in any of these areas others willingly step in.

Secularism is about man being in control, whereas the kingdom is about God being in control. God's control is to be demonstrated through *us, the church, reigning and ruling with Christ in this world.* Secularism exists and rules because not enough Christians understand that Jesus is to be reigning and ruling in our minds (the location of the kingdom) now, and we are, in turn, to be taking dominion over this world as God commanded us since the Garden of Eden. We are not victims of a world gone bad. We are ambassadors of a kingdom that is so powerful it can change even the vilest man or nation. When we begin to understand this and act on it, we will see lives and cultures transformed.

If we are in the kingdom now, why do most, not all, churches say we are not? No church or denomination has perfect revelation or doctrine. The main reason wrong doctrines become entrenched in any church is largely because the individuals in that church have neglected their privilege and responsibility to hear and study God's word for themselves. Denominations were founded on the knowledge they had at the moment and continued to perpetuate. This is not a new phenomenon. Just as the Jews in Jesus' day were stuck in their religious rites, many today are "stuck" in their denominational beliefs, never taking the time to study any of these doctrines for themselves.

Look how much the apostle Paul had to walk away from his belief system. He said, "*...I do not regard myself as having laid hold of it [Christ's teachings] yet; but one thing I do; forgetting what lies behind and reaching forward to what lies ahead*" (Philippians 3:13, NASB). Paul knew he was a work in progress. He was taught in the best schools by the best teachers of his day, yet he was learning that he had to move forward and even discard some of his past training. Likewise, in the kingdom, we need to be constantly learning and studying the Word for ourselves. Second-hand theology is not what God wants for us.

If we are in the kingdom now, what is our responsibility? Every individual in the kingdom of God is responsible morally, physically, mentally and spiritually for themselves. It begins inside every individual, but it should not stay there. The kingdom is to teach you how to run your life, not to let life run you. As you search for and find the kingdom of God in your mind and heart, you can begin to walk it out with your body. You can build on earth the kingdom of heaven and dwell in both worlds.

BUT THERE ARE STILL MORE QUESTIONS!

What about the "end times?" Why do so many events make us believe the world is coming to an end? Even if we are in the kingdom of heaven, why should we be working at ruling and reigning with Christ and making this world a better place if it's all about to end in total destruction?

In the next chapter, we'll continue our study, answering these questions about the end of the world, in addition to discovering what it means to live in the kingdom now and in the future. We do have a hope and a future *on this earth* as well as in eternity.

CHAPTER THREE

WHEN WILL THE END BE?

"...the disciples came to [Jesus] privately, saying, 'Tell us, when shall these things be? And what shall be the sign of Your coming and of the end of the world?'" (Matthew 24:3, NKJV)

CONTINUING OUR TRUTH TREK

Your beliefs affect the choices you make every day, so what you believe about "the end" is very important. We invite you to get out your spiritual thinking cap again as we begin Chapter Three by addressing the questions set forth at the end of Chapter Two - What about the "end times?" Why do so many events make us believe the world is coming to an end? Even if we are in the kingdom of heaven, why should we be working at ruling and reigning with Christ and making this world a better place if it's all about to end in total destruction? Do we have a hope and a future *on this earth,* or just in eternity?

KEYS TO UNDERSTANDING SCRIPTURE

As we begin, let's set out a few basic ground rules for sound biblical investigation, interpretation and good understanding. There are some basic questions we need to ask and tools we need to use.

- We should look at the original languages and words used - Aramaic, Greek and Hebrew - to best determine meaning.
- We need to ask of specific passages - To whom was this written?
- We must discern - Are these verses literal or figurative?
- We should let scripture interpret scripture - The best interpreter of scripture is truly itself.
- We should not be afraid to use other widely recognized valid historical writings of the time - Josephus, Tacitus, Origen, Clement, Seneca, and other accepted historical literature enlarges our understanding and validates scripture.

WHAT DID JESUS SAY ABOUT "THE END"?

Surely one of the most famous conversations about the end times and tribulation that Jesus ever had with his disciples is found in Matthew 24, often called "The Mt. Olivet Discourse." Jesus was approached by His disciples who asked him the question, *"Tell us, <u>when</u> shall these things be? And what shall be <u>the sign</u> of Your coming and of <u>the end of the world</u>?"'* (Matthew 24:3, NKJV). Jesus' detailed answer continues through Chapter 24 and 25 and is worthy of deep investigation (which we strongly urge you to do), but we'll try to briefly summarize three key points:

- the *"signs"*- what they are and when they were to take place;
- *when* "the end" was to occur;
- *what end (of the world)* was Jesus talking about

THE OVERVIEW

Signs - Matthew 24:4-33 is a long list of a horrible nightmare of (*signs*) that Jesus is saying will occur prior to "the end" - *"For then there will be a great tribulation, such as has not occurred since the beginning of the world until now, nor ever will"* (Matthew 24:21, NASB). These events/ signs include - earthquakes, famine, cosmic anomalies (i.e., darkened sun and moon; stars falling from heaven), false prophets, wars, abomination of desolation, destruction of the temple, false Christs, and the one good sign - the gospel preached in all the world.

When - After this frightening and terrible list, Jesus gives his followers a time frame within which to expect these disasters - *"Truly I say to you, this generation will not pass away until all these things take place"* (Matthew 24:34, NASB).

What - Matthew 24 is loaded with phrases about "the end." *"...the end of the world"* (Matthew 24:3, KJV); *"... but the end is not yet"* (Matthew 24:6, KJV); *"...he that shall endure until the end"* (Matthew 24:13, KJV); *"...and then the end shall come"* (Matthew 24:14, KJV). But what exactly is it that was ending?

A CLOSER LOOK – END OF WHAT?

We're going to examine these points - *signs, when and what* - in reverse order for better clarity. First, let's address "what end" Jesus was talking about. Was it really the end of the world - planet Earth ceasing to exist?

There are primarily three Greek words used in the New Testament for "world." *Strong's Concordance* defines them as follows:

- aion (#165) – an age; specifically Jewish or Messianic period
- kosmos (#2889) – the world in a wide or narrow sense, including its inhabitants
- oikoumene (#3625) – land; globe; specifically the Roman Empire

> *"...'And what shall be the sign of Your coming and of the end of the world?'"* (Matthew 24:3, KJV)

This *"end of the world"* is *aion* or the end of an age. What age was ending? The Old Testament, the Old Covenant, the age of animal sacrifice. Christ was in the process of ushering in His Kingdom, the New Testament, the New Covenant. His birth began this process. His one-time sacrifice for all and subsequent resurrection would continue his kingdom. The final fulfillment would be the fall of the Jewish temple system (animal sacrifices ceasing with the destruction of a man-built temple), and His saving gospel message being preached to all the world. This was the *end* of the Old Covenant, and the *coming* of the New Covenant. This *"coming"* His disciples are asking about would mark the actual *end of an age* and beginning of another – not the end of the planet Earth.

Using other scriptures to verify this, we can see the same *"end of the world"* phrase used three times in Matthew 13:38-49 (KJV) when Jesus is explaining the parable of the sower. This *"end of the world"* is again *aion,* or the end of an age, not the end of the physical world. In addition, when Daniel prophesied about these end times, he referred to them as *"the time of the end"* (Daniel 7:17, NKJV), not the end of time. Big difference.

> *"...you shall hear of wars and rumors of wars... all theses things must come to pass, but the end is not yet"* (Matthew 24:6, KJV).

> *"But he that shall endure to the end, the same shall be saved"* (Matthew 24:13, KJV).

> *"This gospel of the kingdom shall be preached in all the world...and then shall the end come"* (Matthew 24:14, KJV).

Jesus is still speaking to the same group of people about the same subject, so it would be a reasonable assumption that He is speaking of the same end of the age, in their day and time, not the end of the world/earth as we know it in our day and time.

In addition, the *"world"* in which the gospel shall be preached (mentioned in Matthew 24:14) is *oikoumene -* specifically the Roman Empire, not the entire earth. The apostle Paul understood this and confirmed that the gospel was preached (past tense) in all the world in separate letters written to the Colossians and the Romans -

"...continue in the faith...be not moved away from the hope of the gospel...which <u>was preached to every creature</u> which is under heaven..." (Colossians 1:23, NKJV).

"Now to Him who is able to establish you according to my gospel and the preaching of Jesus Christ, according to the revelation of the mystery which has been kept secret...but now is manifested and <u>has been made known to all the nations</u>..." (Romans 16:25-26, NASB).

As we define terms and let scripture clarify scripture, it is evident that the "*end*" Jesus was speaking of was the end of the age – the end of the Old Covenant - <u>not</u> the end of the earth. Let's continue and see if this is further verified by the second point...when?

A CLOSER LOOK – WHEN WOULD THIS "END OF AGE" HAPPEN?

"Truly I say to you, <u>this generation</u> will not pass away until all these things take place" (Matthew 24:34, NAS).

This is a direct quote from Jesus. Our goal in understanding scripture should be to view reality as defined by Jesus. If His Lordship means anything, it means He has the right to define our perspective.

In answering the disciples' question about the timing of these calamities and His return, Jesus begins with the phrase, "*Truly I say to you*". Whenever Jesus used these words, it was always to give special emphasis to what followed. Therefore, we must handle this passage with thorough investigation and extraordinary scrutiny.

Some have taught that *"this generation"* really means "race" or "nation" and that Jesus was saying the Jewish race would not die out until all these things took place. Could that be true? Here is a place to begin to honestly ask yourself whether your views on the end times were developed by default (someone else's teaching) or by diligent personal study.

Check your concordance - There are ten passages in Matthew, four in Mark, and 13 in Luke that refer to *"this generation."* Not one of these 27 references is speaking of the entire Jewish race over thousands of years. In addition, Thayer's Greek Lexicon of the New Testament defines generation (Greek - *genea)* as - *The whole multitude of men living at the same time*.

Let's look at the context - Who is Jesus speaking to? The disciples. He said, *"I say to you, this generation..."* In a similar passage, Jesus was again addressing His disciples when He said, *"Truly I say to you, there are some of those who are standing here who will not taste death until they see the Son of Man coming in His kingdom"* (Matthew 16:28, NASB). Are any of the disciples whom Jesus was speaking to alive today? I don't think so! The obvious conclusion is that Jesus arrived in His kingdom while some of the disciples were still living. Either that, or Jesus lied.

The straightforward interpretation of when this *"end of the world/age"* would happen, as simply and clearly stated by Jesus Himself, was within the lifetime of those He was speaking to - His disciples. This leads us to examine the final topic of this pamphlet regarding the *signs* of Christ's return - the events of the tribulation - and when they were to occur.

A CLOSER LOOK – WHAT WILL BE THE SIGNS OF YOUR COMING AT THIS "END OF AGE"?

> *"'Tell us, when shall these things be? And what shall be the sign of Your coming and of the end of the world?'"* (Matthew 24:3, NKJV) *"'Truly I say to you, <u>this generation</u> will not pass away until all these things take place'"* (Matthew 24:34, NASB).

If, as concluded above, Jesus was telling His disciples these signs would happen in *their generation,* then it follows that they would have occurred in their lifetime, and history would record the events of the tribulation (as listed in Matthew 24) - destruction of the temple (verse 2); false Christs (verse 5 and 23); famine and earthquakes (verse 7); delivered to tribulation (verse 9 and 21); false prophets (verse 11 and 24); abomination of desolation (verse 15); cosmic anomalies (i.e., darkened sun and moon; stars falling from heaven – verse 29); and more.

Space will not permit a thorough examination of each of these events, but we will briefly cover a few of them, comparing Christ's statements with trusted historical accounts of events that transpired after His death on the cross until the fall of Jerusalem in 70 A.D. (We are able to time-date these writings due to the rulers who are mentioned in the various texts. We strongly recommend you read these historical references for yourself, so as to see the fulfillment of each of these predictions of Christ.)

Matthew 24:2 - Destruction of the temple –"And now the Romans, judging that it was in vain to spare what was round about the holy house, burnt all those places, as also the remains of the cloisters and the gates, two excepted;

the one on the east side, and the other on the south; both which, however, they burnt afterward."[1] Josephus, *The Wars of the Jews,* Book 6: Chapter 5: Section 2, page 741.

"Now, as soon as the army had no more people to slay or to plunder... Caesar gave orders that they should now demolish the entire city and temple."[2] Josephus, *The Wars of the Jews,* – Book 7: Chapter 1: Section 1, page 750.

Matthew 24:5, 11, 23-24 – False Christs and prophets -"A false prophet was the occasion of these people's destruction, who had made a public proclamation in the city that very day, that God commanded them to get upon the temple, and that there they should receive miraculous signs of their deliverance."[3] Josephus, *The Wars of the Jews,* Book 6: Chapter 5: Section 2, page 741.

Matthew 24:7 – Famine and earthquakes -"Now of those that perished by famine in the city, the number was pro-digious, and the miseries they underwent were unspeak-able; for if so much as the shadow of any kind of food did anywhere appear, a war was commenced presently; and the dearest friends fell a-fighting one with another about it, snatching from each other the most miserable supports of life."[4] Josephus, *The Wars of the Jews,* Book 6: Chapter 3: Section 3, page 737.

"How often have cities in Asia, how often in Achaia, been laid low by a single shock of earthquake! How many towns in Syria, how many in Macedonia, have been swallowed up! How often has this kind of devastation laid Cyprus in ruins! How often has Paphos collapsed! Not infrequently are tidings brought to us of the utter destruction of entire cities."[5] Seneca, *Lucilium Epistulae Morales,* page 180.

Matthew 24:9, 21 – Tribulation - "It is worth appending to it the infallible prediction of our Savior regarding these very things... *'Woe to those who are pregnant and to those who are nursing infants in those days. Pray that your flight may not be in winter or on a Sabbath. For at that time there will be great suffering, such as has not been seen from the beginning of the world until now, no, and never will be [Matt.24:19-21]'.* In estimating the total number of lives lost, the historian [Josephus] says that 1.1 million died by famine and the sword, that the partisans and terrorists informed against each other after the city's capture and were executed, and that the tallest and handsomest of the youths were saved for the triumphal parade. Of the rest, those over seventeen were sent as prisoners to hard labor in Egypt, and even more were divided among the provinces to be killed in the theaters by sword or wild beasts. Those under seventeen were sold into slavery and the number of these alone was ninety thousand. This all happened in the second year of Vespasian's reign in accordance with the prophecies of Christ."[6] Eusebius, *The Church History,* Book 3: Section 7, page 100-101.

Matthew 24:15 – Abomination of Desolation - "We have still to add to our chronology the following...-- I mean the days which Daniel indicates from the desolation of Jerusalem, the seven years and seven months of the reign of Vespasian. For the two years are added to the seventeen months and eighteen days of Otho, and Galba, and Vitellius; and the result is three years and six months, which is "the half of the week," as Daniel the prophet said. For he said that there were two thousand three hundred days from the time that the abomination of Nero stood in the holy city, till its destruction." ⁷ Clement of Alexandria, *The Stromata*, Book 1, Chapter 21.

Matthew 24:29 – Cosmic anomalies (i.e. darkened sun and moon; stars falling from heaven) – This reference is the most complex of all because it has both literal and figurative fulfillments. First of all, such cosmic events have been witnessed throughout history – darkened sun and moon are eclipses – stars falling from the heavens are meteorite showers. Such literal happenings do not, however, indicate the imminent destruction of our universe. In addition, what must be equally considered is the fact that such language is found throughout Biblical prophecy to <u>symbolically</u> describe nations, leaders and earthly events.

Any study of historical writings reveals that many ancient cultures worshipped the sun, moon and stars as gods and interpreted such cosmic anomalies as these listed in Matthew to be a sign of earthly or heavenly disasters and warfare. Moses sternly warned the Israelites against worshiping the sun, moon, stars and all the hosts of heaven (Deuteronomy 4:19; 17:3). Though worshipers of the one true God did stop worshiping the sun, moon and stars, their prophecies still spoke of these heavenly bodies as <u>symbols</u> of headship. This is illustrated by the interpretation of Joseph's dream in which celestial bodies were clearly understood by his family to symbolize themselves –

> *"Now he had still another dream, and related it to his brothers, and said, 'Lo, I have had still another dream; and behold, the sun and the moon and eleven stars were bowing down to me.' And he related it to his father and to his*

brothers; and his father rebuked him and said to him, 'What is this dream that you have had? Shall I and your mother and your brothers actually come to bow ourselves down before you to the ground'?" (Genesis 37:9-10, NASB)

Many other places in Old Testament prophecies spoke of these three entities together – the sun, moon and stars - and any predicted cosmic disturbance of them was under-stood by the hearers of that time (and current scholars) as some form of impending earthly shake-up of one kingdom defeating another -

"The burden of Babylon, which Isaiah the son of Amoz did see... The Lord of hosts musters the host of the battle. Howl, for the day of the Lord is at hand!.... For the <u>stars of heaven and the constellations thereof shall not give their light; the sun shall be darkened in its going forth, and the moon shall not cause her light to shine</u>. I will punish the world for their evil.... Behold, I will stir up the Medes against them." (Isaiah 13:1-17, NKJV)

History records the Median empire conquered Babylon in 538 BC and this prophecy by Isaiah could be most logically interpreted - through the lens of history - to be predicting the falling of one empire and rising of another, rather than speaking of literal heavenly events.

So when Jesus uses <u>these exact words</u>, with the order slightly changed, he is using Isaiah's specific verbiage, which He knew His disciples would understand as pro-phetic symbolism, to refer to the fall of Jerusalem in the lifetime of His hearers. Jerusalem (Israel) was going to be destroyed in the same way as Babylon was six centuries before. This is a great example of letting scripture interpret scripture, rather than misinterpreting ancient, figurative language as literal, modern day disasters.

Consider it from a modern-day standpoint: Someone reads the front page of the newspaper and learns that lions attacked some ranchers in Montana. The ranchers are badly injured and end up in the hospital. The reader has some feeling of compassion. He then turns to the sports page and reads that the Tigers killed the Cowboys. The reader either rejoices, mourns or yawns. It was a football game. Then he turns to the editorial section and argues with the opinions of the writer. He might later read the comics and laugh. All of these are in the same newspaper, yet each is interpreted in light of the kind of literature it is. Surely we can and should employ the same level of discernment and scrutiny in our reading and understanding of scripture.

IN SUMMARY

In Chapter Two – The Kingdom – we set forth Jesus' bold statement that the Kingdom of God is within you (Luke 17:20-21) and therefore, on this earth here and now. In this chapter – When Will the End Be? – we have again quoted Jesus and carefully evaluated the context and content of His statement to determine that this earth is not about to end in tribulation and destruction.

We cannot overemphasize our desire to encourage you to honor and obey the scripture that says, *"Be diligent [study] to present yourself approved to God, a worker who does not need to be ashamed, rightly dividing the word of truth"* (2 Timothy 2:15, NKJV). Don't settle for "second-hand theology." Don't let someone else tell you what to believe (including this book). Our goal is to stimulate your hunger and facilitate your search for truth – correct interpretation and application of God's Word. Christ longs to develop a relationship that comes from you learning directly from Him.

The teaching of believers being rescued from this world so it can be destroyed does not do justice to the redeeming work of Christ. He has given us all the necessary equipment to be victorious in this world. This teaching short-changes the power of the cross and the resurrection. We are not victims of a world gone bad. We are ambassadors of a kingdom that is so powerful it can change even the vilest man or nation. This message of the kingdom is so full of *hope* it can create faith that not only moves mountains, but can transform cultures.

What we hope for determines our attitudes, beliefs and actions. There are undesirable consequences for wrong thoughts or hopes just as surely as there are awesome blessings for right thoughts and hopes. Hope is a bridge that can lead to either dismay and surrender or courage and victory. What we hope for is incredibly important. As believers, our hopes are two-fold, encompassing both physical life on this earth as well as an eternal spiritual life. What is it you hope for in each of these realms?

In the next chapter we'll continue our study to help you search out your personal answer to this very important question that will literally determine your daily activities and ultimate destiny – *Just what is it you hope for?*

CHAPTER FOUR

WHAT IS IT YOU "HOPE" FOR?

...[I, Paul] do not cease...making mention of you in my prayers: that the God of our Lord Jesus Christ...may give you a spirit of wisdom and revelation in the knowledge of Him. I pray that the eyes of your heart may be enlightened so that you will know what is the <u>hope of His calling</u>...(Ephesians 1:16-18, NKJV)

A BRIEF REVIEW

As we continue our "truth trek" let's remember the foundation that was established in chapters two and three:

- Chapter Two – Jesus prayed that God's kingdom should *come on earth* so His will could be *done on earth* in the same way it is done in heaven (Matthew 6:10). He further declared that the kingdom of God is *within believers* (Luke 17:20-21). The obvious conclusion is that if something is *within* believers and our bodies are here on this earth, then that which is *in* believers is necessarily also located *on* this earth. Therefore, the kingdom of heaven is here on this earth now.

- Chapter Three – We again quoted Jesus in relation to "When Will the End Be?", evaluated the context and content of His statements and determined that this earth is not about to end in tribulation and destruction. Rather, he was speaking of the *end* of one age – the old covenant of animal sacrifice – and the *beginning* of another age – the new covenant of Christ's one-time sacrificial death for all.

These two conclusions inescapably bring up many more questions. First and foremost, what is the role of believers on this earth, here and now, if the kingdom of God is here and the world is not about to cease to exist? If our primary *hope* has been to escape the coming tribulation and be with God in heaven forever, what are we to do with that?

Be encouraged! We do not need to lose our hope. We do need to re-evaluate it.

THE IMPORTANCE OF HOPE

As stated at the conclusion of Chapter Three, what we hope for is incredibly important. The *hope* of scripture is of inestimable significance as it relates to both our daily duties and ultimate destiny in this life and the one to come.

There are undesirable consequences for wrong thoughts and false hopes just as surely as there are awesome blessings for right thoughts and true hopes. False hope is a rickety bridge that will lead to fear, dismay and surrender.

True hope is a solid, strong bridge that will lead to courage, gratification and victory. For this reason it is of utmost importance to carefully and prayerfully examine that for which we hope.

AN OVERVIEW OF SCRIPTURAL HOPE

Let's look at some examples of *hope.* There are nearly 150 references to *hope* in the Bible, so it is obviously a subject God cares about a lot. The length and scope of this booklet will only allow a small sampling investigation, but the authors' *hope* is that you, the reader, will be sufficiently inspired to continue your own personal study of this essential topic and honestly ask yourself - Are these the things that I hope for?

- *"This* [rich and glorious] *secret is Christ Himself, who is in you. He is our only <u>hope</u> for glory"* (Colossians 1:27, NCV).

BASIC CONCLUSION - Christ in us <u>is</u> (present, not future tense) our hope for glory.

- *"I pray you will...know the <u>hope</u> to which He has called us"* (Ephesians 1:18, NCV).

BASIC CONCLUSION - We must gain knowledge (a clear and certain perception of truth) of the <u>hope of our calling</u>.

- *"We want each of you to go on with the same hard work all your lives, so you will surely get what you <u>hope</u> for"* (Hebrews 6:11, NCV).

BASIC CONCLUSION - We must work hard to be sure to get that for which we hope, which would also imply we have power to achieve our hopes.

- *"We have this <u>hope</u> as an anchor for the soul, sure and strong"* (Hebrews 6:19, NCV).

BASIC CONCLUSION - The right hope is certain and powerful to our soul.

- *"<u>Hope</u> deferred makes the heart sick..."* (Proverbs 13:12, NAS). BASIC CONCLUSION - The wrong hope will make you despondent and depressed.

<u>HOPE DEFINED</u>

What a list! And how many questions are raised in just this short list! Let's begin the deeper search, attempting to clarify and personalize some of these facets of Biblical hope.

First step – define hope. The Greek New Testament word for hope has only two references in <u>Strong's Concordance</u> – a verb and a noun - and one refers to the other. So, biblical hope is very straightforward with singular meaning – *to expect, trust, confide* (verb); *anticipate (usually with pleasure); expectation or confidence* (noun). The <u>American Dictionary of the English Language</u> says hope is – *Confidence in a future event; the highest degree of well founded expectation of good; as hope founded on God's gracious promises.*

Next, let's look individually at the above "hope" scriptures.

HOPE FOR GLORY – Colossians 1:27

This scripture refers to Christ Himself as our only *hope for glory*. I believe this is to be our *first hope*, but to understand it we have to know – What is glory? I love the <u>American Dictionary of the English Language</u> definition:

* Glory - *honorable representation of God. (etymology sense: clear, open, plain, expanse, shining, bright, enlarge)*

In other words, our only hope, the only way we can expect to be an "honorable representation of God" is through Christ being <u>in</u> us. How does this happen? In Matthew 3, John the Baptist tells us how. He preached repentance – to change your heart and life.

We choose to talk to Christ and ask forgiveness for where we have missed the mark. We invite Him into our lives, acknowledging our inability to become an "honorable representation of God" without His help.

To sincerely go through this mental and spiritual (not physical) process is to become a child of God – to be born again and enter the kingdom of heaven *while we are on this earth*. This is a spiritual kingdom, ruled by Christ as the King of this kingdom. Because it is a spiritual kingdom, the only way it can be entered is through our minds, our thoughts, and our spirits submitting to Christ as our King, our ruler. But then what? After this hope is fulfilled, is there more?

The etymology sense of the word glory indicates there is much more – more clarity, more openness, a bigger expanse, brightness and enlarging – growing in our becoming an honorable representation of God. This is another facet of the *hope* we are to embrace and leads us to the next verse.

THE HOPE OF HIS CALLING – Ephesians 1:18

This scripture declares we need to know the *hope* to which we are called. The word *called* is a very personal, by name calling. God calls us, by name, and it is for a reason, an expectation – there is a *hope* in our calling. What is that hope? Is it just to be born again so as to spend spiritual eternity with Him, or is there more to it? Paul was praying in this passage that our understanding would be clarified so we would know what His calling is. This calling and hope must be investigated, prayed for, to learn what it is. So let's take a closer look.

To be born again is to become God's child, part of His family. Why would God want us to be His child? For many of the same reasons earthly parents have children: Because He loves us, wants to have an intimate relationship with us, and He has a plan for our lives. In the same way an earthly parent has love, expectations or hopes for each of their children, God has *hope* for what we will become as we grow up and mature. God cares for, teaches and provides us with all we need to do so. Let's look at hope from a parent's perspective in the natural world.

As parents, we have great hopes (expectations) for our children and they all involve growth – physical and spiritual. We care for, teach and provide what they need along the way to attain this growth. We hope they will learn to walk and when they do, our hope changes and moves up to the next stage of development – talking, potty training, etc. We also hope for their mental and spiritual growth – thinking, reasoning and making good, Godly choices. In other words, character development that will make them more and more into an "honorable representation of God."

As they mature properly, they will develop their own set of hopes – some physical and some spiritual. As a parent, my *hope* for my children is fulfilled as they *hope* for the right things. If they fail to mature or hope for wrong things my heart aches because I know they will be hurt to whatever degree they are either off course with their hopes or they do not walk out their God-ordained journey.

I am confident these emotions and outcomes must be similar to God and how He relates to us as a loving parent to His child. My greatest desire would be to teach my child to seek and learn <u>what</u> to hope for, how to seek and find God's will on their own so their desires can be fulfilled as their God-given paths are discovered and walked out. Accuracy in what we hope for cannot be overstated. It is the major player of our life outcomes.

Do you know the hope of His calling in your life? What gifts has He given you, and how are you to use them? For God surely calls us to serve others, not just to be saved. Let's continue the search.

<u>WORK TO GET WHAT YOU HOPE FOR –</u> <u>Hebrews 6:11</u>

The next scripture declares we are to "*<u>go on</u> with the same hard work all our lives so you will surely get what you <u>hope</u> for.*" This would seem to indicate that we are not to hope for a single event, but rather that hope is an <u>ongoing</u> process that requires work. Could this be what Paul was speaking of in 2 Corinthians 3:18 when he said "*...we...are being transformed into the same image* [the

Lord's] *from glory to glory"* becoming an ever improving "honorable representation of God"?

So, back to the question of this chapter – *What is it you hope for?* Are you hoping for the right thing? Does your hope take you from glory to glory? Does your hope lead you to "expect something with pleasure and confidence?" Does your hope lead you to grow in your Christian walk, to go from a newborn baby in the faith to an increasingly strong and capable son of God?

When I learned of my need for Jesus, my immediate hope was for salvation – to be born again. I got it – hope fulfilled. Now what? I wanted to serve God, so I hoped to learn and receive my spiritual gift. I learned it was teaching. Got it – hope fulfilled. Now what? Go on. I hoped to use my gift. I began studying to develop my gift, writing and teaching, even getting a book published and a speaking tour to promote it. Got it – hope fulfilled. Now what do I hope for? Go on. Continue to grow up, using my gift and time wisely and learning more and teaching more.

This growth takes me deeper into my mind and heart – where hope lives and the kingdom of heaven is found – to study and get to know God more intimately. I believe this is the hard work spoken of in this third scripture – Hebrews 6:11 – working hard to be certain to attain that for which we hope – to be an honorable representation of God. It is intentionally using and developing my inborn, natural qualities and spiritual gifts to serve others.

In other words, *hope* is an ongoing growth process, achieving one hope and then going on to the next, and then on to the next. Remember the definition – *to antici-pate (usually with pleasure); hope founded on God's gra-cious promises.* Begin to learn what God's promises are and you'll begin to learn what to hope for. God's hope takes us from glory to glory – an ever expanding spiritual territory, expanse of knowledge, mental enlightenment.

Hope is not a destination any more than glory is an achievement. Hope is a journey that takes you from glory to glory to glory. Hope is going on and ongoing – to the next hope, to the next glory. Hope is not looking back. Hope is going forward, growing up, going on, knowing there will always be more to be hoped for after we reach that which we are hoping for today.

TRUE HOPE – Hebrews 6:19 vs FALSE HOPE – Proverbs 13:12

We must ask again – *What is it you hope for? Are you hoping for the right thing?* These two scriptures contrast the difference between right hope and wrong hope. It's pretty stark. One brings strength to your soul. The other brings sickness to your heart.

Hoping for the right thing is essential to deepening our relationship with Jesus because what you hope for is *"expected, anticipated with pleasure and confidence."* If hope is deferred or delayed, it brings doubt into the relationship. If hope is actually removed because of seeing events unfold in completely the "wrong" way, relationships can be utterly destroyed and hearts broken.

The consequences of wrong hope range from devastating to deadly. Here are two graphic and dramatic historical examples:

During Jesus's triumphal entry into Jerusalem just before Passover, the people present were praising God for giving them a <u>k</u>ing who would be an earthly, national leader. Few understood he was <u>The King</u> who was establishing an entirely new, spiritual kingdom. They were hoping for the wrong thing. The tragic result was most of them who were praising Him earlier were screaming for His death by crucifixion just a few hours later. We'll never know how many lives were ruined and hearts crushed as a result.

Forty years later in 70 A.D. we do know from the writings of Josephus, a first century Jewish historian, that 1.1 million Jews were horrifically slaughtered in Jerusalem because they were still dwelling under the false hope of the Messiah's coming as a future event.

These are powerful examples of Proverbs 13:12 – *"Hope deferred makes the heart sick..."* Strong's Concordance defines heart and sick as follows:

- Heart – *feelings, will, intellect.*
- Sick – *worn out, weak, grieve, in pain, wounded in travail; labor with pain.*

The consequences of false hope can wound your feelings, will and intellect. This is your soul – *"the part of man that enables him to think and reason"* (American Dictionary of the English Language) – and it can devastate it to the point of wearing you out, bringing physical pain so strong as to be called travail. This kind of mental anguish is destructive both physically and spiritually and can totally alter your belief system; i.e. from worshiping Jesus to demanding His death. Continuing on this path of wrong hope led to the largest human massacre the world has ever known (based proportionally on the world population then and now).

True hope, on the other hand, is described at the end of Proverbs 13:12 (NKJV) – *"...but when the desire [hope] comes it is a tree of life."* <u>Strong's Concordance</u> defines this tree of life as:

- Tree of life - *Strong, well-watered, firm plant; merry; joyful, exhilarated to laughter, delightful.*

This is the hope God desires for us.

WHAT HOPE DO YOU CHOOSE?

Do you have this kind of hope – that which brings joy and delight? Is this the kind of hope that is engendered when we are taught to expect the world to get worse and worse until we are finally taken out of the mess? Where has this kind of defeatist hope taken us? By and large, the church has retreated from the world, meeting on Sunday morning for some good advice from scripture, then back to the work-a-day world with little thought and less action to impact it for and with Christ. The few who do share Christ usually do so with the goal of evangelism, with no accompanying discipling on how to take dominion of this earth as we have been commanded to do. Why polish the deck chairs on the Titanic?

On the other hand, seeking and finding the "hope of His calling" will lead us to mature as sons of God and propel us to appropriate action. We are called to be like Christ. Did He seek to escape the world or work to heal it? When faced with the greatest challenge of His life, Jesus prayed in the garden of Gethsemane for God to remove the frightful suffering before Him, if possible. Did God remove it? No. However, Jesus also prayed for the Father's will to be done, not His. If God did not relieve Jesus of the worst suffering His son could endure, why do we think

He would remove us from this world instead of helping us transform it?

SO WHAT ARE WE TO DO WITH THIS HOPE?

Let's look a little deeper to see who God says we are and what we are to do. 1 Peter 2:9 speaks of believers as "royal priests." What is royalty? A king. What does a king do? He rules over his kingdom. What does a priest do? He attends to the things of God. The clear implication of being royal priests, therefore, is to rule in righteousness. Ruling in righteousness is hard work, requiring both power and authority. Good news: 2 Timothy 2:12 speaks of reigning (ruling) with Christ. This means we don't have to do it alone! (For those who think this scripture refers to the next life, what would there be to rule over in a heaven where all is perfect?)

So which is it you hope for? To escape from this world or to rule it? You can't have it both ways. One leads to despair and hopelessness and is totally without power - impotent. The other leads to victory and joy through God-given power and authority. Which one sounds more like God's plan: to wait quietly to escape the battle or to enter the battle and win? Were you born-again to be ready to leave this earth or ready to serve on it and rule over it?

But where do we get this power? More good news: We do not need to wait for the return of Christ to begin ruling and reigning with Him or to be empowered. Christ already returned several times after His resurrection, but the visitation that brought about our empowering was at Pentecost in the form of the Holy Spirit. His spiritual presence within believers today is far more empowering than any fleshly return in the future would be. Flesh is limited to its location. Spirit has no such limitations.

God's hope is empowering. Any hope that takes us down is wrong hope and is not from God. We cannot change this world if we do not hope for a better one. Ruling in righteousness is hard work. Do we even know how or where to start? God is waiting for each of His children to come to a better understanding of who He is and who we are *in* Him so that He can work through us as surely and strongly as He worked through Jesus.

God put us here, planted us on this earth, so that we would bear fruit. We are in the middle of an opportunity to re-make society. Do you hope to be able to step up to the plate and re-make it according to God's plan? Or do you simply hope to escape and let someone else clean it up? Are you growing up and maturing into a "son of God" or are you still a newborn baby, simply born-again?

WALKING OUT HOPE –BECOMING SONS OF GOD

Our greatest hope should be to become sons of God. Christ was the first-born son. We are to become like our big brother. In the gospel of John, he writes about how and why Christ came to earth – that *"...as many as received Him, to them He gave <u>power to become</u> the sons of God, even to them that believe on his name"* (John 1:12, KJV). Christ's purpose on this earth was to give those who believe on His name the *power to become* the sons of God.

Later, John declares *"...now we are children* [sons] *of God; and it has not yet been revealed what we shall be, but we know that <u>when He is revealed, we shall be like Him</u>...* (1 John 3:2, NKJV). This is powerful and re-affirms our "hope for glory" (Colossians 1:27) lies in the fact that becoming an honorable representation of God is a process of getting to know Him better. *"When He is revealed"* – the more we get to know Him – *"we shall be like Him."*

This brings us full circle back to the original verse in this chapter - *"...[I, Paul] do not cease...making mention of you in my prayers: that the God of our Lord Jesus Christ...may give you a <u>spirit of wisdom and revelation in the knowledge of Him</u>. I pray that the eyes of your heart may be enlightened so that you will know what is the <u>hope of His calling</u>..."*(Ephesians 1:16-18, NKJV)

Our primary goal in life is to <u>grow in the knowledge of Christ</u>. When we do, we begin to learn the <u>hope of His calling</u> – the path and objective for which God created each of us. As we go through this process, we grow from born-again babies into sons of God, learning and beginning to walk out our purpose in power and authority – *the <u>hope</u> of glory – going from glory to glory*. There's important, fulfilling work to be done in the kingdom, and we all have a part in it.

<u>WHERE AND HOW DO I BEGIN?</u>

In the next chapter we are going to begin to learn what it means to be a son of God. Who am I? What am I to do? Where am I to do it? How am I to do it? These are profound, personal questions and learning the answers will lead to your true identity in Christ and purpose for being. It can plant the biggest and truest *hope* your heart has ever had. Please stay with us on this wonderful journey.

God's promise spoken to Jeremiah is still valid to His sons today: *"...'I know what I am planning for you,' says the Lord. 'I have good plans for you, not plans to hurt you. I will give you <u>hope</u> and a <u>good future</u>'"*(Jeremiah 29:11, NCV).

CHAPTER FIVE

SONS OF GOD – WHO ARE THEY & HOW ARE THEY LIKE JESUS?

"...as many as received Him, to them He gave <u>power to become the sons of God</u>, even to them that believe on his name" (John 1:12, KJV).

"...now we are children [<u>sons</u>] of God; and it has not yet been revealed what we shall be, but we know that when He is revealed, we shall be like Him... (1 John 3:2, NKJV).

THOUGHTS MATTER

With each chapter we have encouraged the reader to put on their spiritual thinking cap. We do so again! For the biggest battle we all face is over what we think and believe. The battle is *in* us.

It is our thoughts that lead us to believe we are either preparing to escape this world, or we are commissioned to make it a more beautiful place to live. Our job is to align our thoughts with God's thoughts so we can work out His desires for this world. We need to be willing to study the Word with an open mind and heart. This means we will be ready to change the way we think if it is revealed that our thoughts are in opposition to God's revealed plans.

The church needs to train soldiers to identify the true battlefront: *"We are taking every <u>thought captive</u> to the obedience of Christ..."* (2 Corinthians 10:5, NASB). To take a "thought captive" is to take a prisoner and it means we are at war within our minds. Thoughts enter the mind, go through the spirit and come out in action in the flesh. The first enemy we must fight is the one within us - wrong thoughts. The enemy is anything or anyone who takes our *mind* off Jesus and His purpose for us.

Taking thoughts captive is no small task as it often means foundational changes in our thinking! So, strap on that spiritual thinking cap again, and let's enter the deep waters of learning who the sons of God are, and how they become like Christ.

SOLIDIFYING THE FOUNDATION

Our chapters two, three and four have led us to some heavy duty thoughts, as we studied God's Word in context and with definitions:

- Chapter Two - The kingdom of heaven is here on this earth now (Luke 17:20-21).
- Chapter Three - Planet earth is not about to end in utter destruction (Matthew 24).
- Chapter Four - True hope is based on going from *glory to glory* (2 Corinthians 3:18) – becoming an

ever-improving "honorable representation of God" –
a son of God.

We finished Chapter Four with the scriptures in the
title of this volume, introducing the idea of becoming a
son of God as our greatest hope. *"...as many as received
Him, to them He gave <u>power to become</u> the sons of God,
even to them that believe on his name"* (John 1:12, KJV).
Christ was the first-born son. We are to become like our
big brother.

Later, John describes a growth or maturing process of
the sons of God - *"...now we are children* [sons] *of God; and
it has not yet been revealed what we shall be, but we know
that <u>when He is revealed, we shall be like Him</u>...* (1 John
3:2, NKJV). This is powerful and re-affirms our "hope for
glory" (Colossians 1:27) lies in the fact that becoming an
honorable representation of God is a process of getting to
know Him better. *"When He is revealed"* – the more we get
to know Him – *"we shall be like Him."*

SONS OF GOD - GROWING UP IN THE KINGDOM

We all enter this natural world born as babies. Babies
grow up as they go through childhood. If they are properly
taught and nurtured by their parents, children mature
into young adults that can be trusted with increasing
amounts of responsibility as they grow. Our spiritual
growth should mirror this natural and nurtured growth.

When we first enter the kingdom of heaven we are
born-again, brand new babies. We are to "grow up" spiritually as evidenced by the many scriptural references
to "children of God." Similar to our natural growth, if we
have been properly taught and nurtured spiritually in the

ways of God, children of God will grow up and mature into *sons of God.*

If we are to truly understand this term – *sons of God* - there are three very important foundational points to consider. As noted in previous volumes, one of the keys to understanding scripture is using the original languages (Aramaic, Greek and Hebrew). By doing so, we first of all learn that *sons of God* is not a gender term, but simply means offspring, either a son or daughter. Since we are looking at a spiritual relationship, this makes perfect sense as scripture declares that in the kingdom of heaven there is neither male nor female (Galatians 3:28).

Second, the original Aramaic language used the phrase *son of God* and it was often [mis]translated to *children of God* in our modern Bibles. To the authors of scripture the significance and difference between *children of God* and *sons of God* was very important, relating specifically to maturity and responsibility. A child does not think for himself. He depends on his parents. A mature son has learned how to start thinking for himself and is making adult decisions and doing adult jobs (Galatians 4:1-7).

This is demonstrated today in the Jewish celebrations of bar mitzvah (for boys) and bat mitzvah (for girls), both of which occur at age 13. Prior to this ceremony, the parents hold the responsibility for the child's adherence to law and tradition. After this age children bear their own responsibility for law, tradition and ethics.

This is a carry-over from Jesus' day. In first century Jewish culture, this age was also a dividing line between childhood and adulthood. In Luke 2:41-49 we read the story of 12-year-old Jesus remaining in the temple in Jerusalem after Passover rather than returning home with His family. When He is questioned by his earthly parents about this decision He tells them, *"I must be about my Father's business."* Jesus understood that he had reached the age of a *son of God* who must now bear his own responsibility for law, tradition and ethics – being about His Father's business.

Third, if we are to truly grasp what it is to be a *son of God* it is incumbent to have a working definition of who our Father is. Defining God in His infinity and fullness is an impossibility, but nevertheless, still useful to our objective. The <u>American Dictionary of the English Language</u> is best suited for this task. It is the book we've used most often for this series, is also known as <u>Webster's 1828</u>, and was America's very first dictionary. It was compiled and researched by founding father Noah Webster, a recognized Bible scholar and master of 27 languages. Unless noted otherwise, all definitions are coming from this source due to its scholarly and Biblical nature.

In addition to definitions, Noah Webster also examined the etymology of words. There are times when the etymology is even more revealing than the definition itself, for it is describing the root or history of a word. This root or primary sense undergirds the entire definition, bringing more meaning or deeper understanding and better application. This is most certainly the case when reading the etymology of the word God - *Except the word Jehovah, I have found the name of the Supreme Being to be usually taken from His supremacy or power and to be equivalent to lord or ruler, from the root signifying to press or exert force.*

Since God is a Spirit Being, it's also important to note that Webster declares – *the primary sense of the word spirit is to rush or drive.*

The truly awesome, exciting, sobering and mind-boggling aspect of these definitions – *supreme power pressing forward and exerting force* - is how they relate to us, as sons of God – who we are and how we become more like Him!

CREATED IN GOD'S IMAGE (Old Testament)

"And God said, 'Let us make man in our <u>image</u>, after our <u>likeness</u>: and let them have dominion... (Genesis 1:26). <u>Strong's Concordance</u> defines image as – *a phantom; resemblance; a representative figure.*

God made me (and all of mankind) to be a "representative figure" of Him. To better understand this, let's look at an example in civil government. I vote to elect my federal representative in Congress and I am upset if he does not perform or vote in the way I want (Constitutionally). I call and write him to advise him how he can better represent me. To project this relationship to the way God created me is to see the overview of God's purpose for creating man in general, but I must take it personally as well:

I am to be God's representative on this earth. He made the earth and everything in it, but giving me dominion over it means I am to replenish it, to rule and manage it in the way He would rule and manage it. I must communicate with Him and hear and honor His desires if I'm to be a good representative.

For greater understanding of what and who I am, let's define a few more terms.

The first word in <u>Strong's Concordance</u> defining "image" was *phantom*.

- phantom – *something that appears, an apparition; a <u>specter</u>; a visible spirit.*

- specter – *something made preternaturally visible (in a manner beyond or aside from the common order of nature).*

I'm also made after His "likeness" which <u>Strong's</u> defines as – *resemblance, manner.*

- resemblance – *similitude either of external form or of qualities; a resemblance in manners or disposition.*
- manner – *form; method, way of performing or executing; custom; habitual practice.*

THINKING THROUGH IT ALL

Pulling all these definitions together is very revealing. First of all, the essence of being created in God's image is spirit in nature as the first word in <u>Strong's</u> that defines image is *phantom*. But the interesting thing about the definitions that arise from phantom is the <u>un-natural</u> manifestation. For though a phantom is a specter, which we would think of as a ghost, the definition declares a specter is "preternaturally visible." In other words, the true nature of a specter is to be invisible, but God's image, in which we are created, is a phenomenon aside from the common order of nature in that it is <u>visible</u>. The definition goes so far as to say "a visible spirit" – a seeming contradiction in terms.

So what is it that makes an invisible spirit visible? I believe it is the visible actions that proceed from the invisible spirit. Though the actual spirit may be invisible, the nature of what we are doing – the visible action – is often readily and easily linked to good (e.g., helping those in need) or evil (e.g. stealing a car, beating a child).

Being created in the image of God also means I am to resemble Him in my *manner* and *disposition*. Because I was created by God and in the image of God, it is His spirit that is in me from conception. God is holy. God is good. God is loving, kind, compassionate, patient, just. In addition, because I am created in His spirit image, by definition I have God's *rush or drive to exert force and power* as a ruler – the primary sense of God. The very nature of my being created in the image of God's spirit makes me physically and spiritually <u>capable</u> of ruling like God.

These are governmental terms and fit with the command by God that I am to take dominion (govern) over all He has created – earth and all creatures. I must first govern/rule myself in the same way God governs Himself if I am to be a *representative figure* for Him on this earth.

The Bible is the textbook from which to learn all I can about God and His character. As I learn about *His* character, I am seeing how He wants *me* to be, for He made me in His image to be like Him, to rule like Him, to be holy, loving, kind, compassionate like Him.

But ruling also involves right judgment and exercising power and authority over any and all things that are not aligned with God and His word, His character and how He would care for/rule the earth. Being like God involves love, but that love is not always "touchy-feel good" love. It includes much discipline and power to enforce what is right by punishing that which is wrong, if we are to govern properly.

- Govern – *to control or restrain; keep in due subjection, as to govern passions or temper. To direct and control the actions or conduct of men by established law; regulate by authority. To keep within the limits of prescribed law.*

God has given his sons the spirit of *power, love and a sound mind* (2 Timothy 1:7). This is the way I was created, with the ability to control myself according to God's standard of power and love. I also have the inborn ability to govern the world as a representative figure of God.

But simply having the ability to do something does not make it happen. I have the ability to read, but someone had to teach me how and I had to choose to use and improve this ability. It was a process – learning letters, then blends and ultimately words. I have the ability to think right thoughts and do right things. But I must choose to learn what they are, to read and study *right things* to feed my spirit properly in order to *develop* the discipline of thinking right thoughts from which right actions proceed. This is developing Godly character. This is becoming a son of God. Let's further investigate this character by progressing to the New Testament.

SONS OF GOD - BEING LIKE JESUS (New Testament)

Now let's relate this to Jesus and our becoming sons of God. *"... it has not yet been revealed what we shall be, but we know that <u>when He is revealed, we shall be like Him</u>...* (1 John 3:2, NKJV).

Scripture is all about revealing Jesus to us. Let's have a look and see one way in which Christ is "revealed" and how that relates to us and our character and our becoming sons of God - "[Jesus] *being the <u>brightness</u> of His* [God's] <u>glory</u> *and the <u>express image</u> of His* [God's] *person..."* (Hebrews 1:3, NKJV).

Once again, we're going to define the terms underlined, and even build a "tree of terms" by using words within the original and ensuing definitions. This will greatly enhance our understanding of this critical and awesome subject – being a son of God.

BRIGHTNESS

We'll begin with <u>Strong's Concordance</u> definition of brightness: (note – [ ] mark my comments within the defintions.)

- Brightness – [used only once in all of Scripture] – *an off flash; i.e.* <u>*effulgence*</u>*, a separation, completion or reversal; (comp. of 575 & 826) – a separation, completion or reversal* [like a mirror reflection]; *to beam forth; shine.*

Now we'll use <u>Webster's 1828</u> to define *effulgence* and a tree of terms within it.

- Effulgence – *flood of light; great luster or brilliance;* <u>*splendor*</u>*. A word of superlative signification, applied with peculiar propriety to the sun and to the Supreme Being.*
- Splendor – *to cast rays; great brightness, brilliant luster; great show of richness and elegance;* <u>*eminence*</u>*.*
- Eminence – *elevation; rising or projecting beyond the rest; a place or station above men in general* [to the point of] *making him conspicuous* [i.e. others will see and recognize his prominence].

Now let's pull these definitions and thoughts together: Jesus Christ, as the Son of God, is an off-flash of God's glory. He is separate and yet part of God's completeness. His glory is so identical as to be like a mirror reflection beaming forth with a brilliance reserved for God only. Light is energy. As bright as this light is for illuminating expansive areas, it can also be a beam or ray to pinpoint or expose focused power or light on a particular point or area. This great show of light and richness emanating from the Son of God (Jesus) set Him not just apart, but *above* men in general and this was obvious – *conspicuous* – to those around Him.

The overwhelming application is how this applies to us as sons of God –

> *"God knew [the people He called] before He made the World and He decided that they would be like his Son, so that Jesus would be the first-born of many brothers. God planned for them to be like his Son..."* (Romans 8:29-30, NCV).

Think about that amazing statement! God planned for the people He called to be like his firstborn Son, Jesus. As a son of God, these descriptions and definitions above of brightness, effulgence, splendor and eminence are what God planned for us to be! This is why we must <u>grow up</u> from being a born-again <u>child</u> of God into a mature son of God. Incredibly, yet literally, this gives us the access and ability to be bright light, richness, elevation, splendor, to begin reflecting as an off-flash of our Father.

GLORY

The next word from the Hebrews passage is "glory." Jesus is the *reflection/ brightness of God's glory.* We'll first look at <u>Strong's Concordance</u> and then <u>Webster's 1828</u> –

- Glory – *dignity, honor (root 1380 – be of reputation)*
- Glory – *honorable representation of God. (etymology sense: clear, open, plain expanse, shining, bright, enlarge).*

To reflect God's glory is to present an honorable representation of Him. The essence or sense of this *glory* is clarity, not confusion. It is open and plain. It has no hidden agenda. It is enlarged and expansive to the point that it can never be totally apprehended or comprehended, though we should always continue trying to do so. It is so bright and shining that the only other word used with this description of brightness is the sun, which will blind you if you try to look at it directly.

God's glory is so big, so bright, that even though it is open to us, we could never take it all in, yet we are to reflect it – mirror it – to the world. This has to be possible or God would not declare it to be so or ask us to do it. It is because we are created in His image/nature that we have this *potential,* and it requires we study and apply His word if we are to walk out this glory in any degree.

EXPRESS IMAGE

Express image, like the word *brightness,* only appears one time in the entire Bible. This makes it of very particular and specific significance, deserving of special

attention to understand it. Once again, we'll start with
<u>Strong's Concordance</u> –

- Express image – *engraver – tool or person. Engraving
  <u>character</u> to an exact copy. (from 5482 – to sharpen
  to a point by scratching or writing. Military application – a <u>palisade</u> or <u>rampart</u>, a mound for <u>circumval-
  lation</u> in a siege.)*

To further clarify and investigate, we'll use
<u>Webster's 1828</u> -

- Character – *a mark made by cutting or engraving,
  a stone or other hard material. The* [singular] *peculiar qualities, impressed by nature* [inborn] *or habit*
  [learned] *on a person which distinguish him from
  others. These* [inborn, natural qualities] *constitute
  <u>real character</u>; and the qualities which he is <u>sup-
  posed to possess</u> constitute his <u>estimated character</u>
  or reputation* [the qualities gained by habit]. *Hence,
  we say a character is not formed when the person
  has not <u>acquired</u> stable and distinctive qualities.*

Once again, let's pull this together as it relates to being
a son of God. Jesus Christ being *the express image of
God* is all about His character. By definition, character
is both inborn/natural and also learned or gained by
habit. In addition, it declares that forming character is a
violent, difficult process, illustrated by the fact that the
engraved mark is accomplished by cutting or sharpening
hard material.

Secondly, there are two aspects to character – one is
inborn and one can be learned. In other words, Jesus

possesses the character of God because He was born that way. But the other side of Christ's character is that His flesh was created with the <u>potential</u> to have His habits formed in such a way as to <u>become</u> an "exact copy" of His heavenly Father. To be created in this type of *image* has nothing to do with what we look like on the outside and everything to do with what we truly are like, and <u>think</u> like on the inside.

By definition, even though the qualities must be an *exact image* of God, they are still singular, unique to the individual. This is surely a wonderful example of God's infinity - that an immeasurable number of individuals can be formed in God's express image, with each and every one still maintaining their unique individuality…amazing.

So, how did Jesus learn to acquire God's character traits? For *real character* is what distinguishes us from others and *estimated character* is what we are supposed to possess, that which we are working towards learning. Scripture answers this clearly:

> *"Even though Jesus Christ was the son of God,*
> *he <u>learned</u> obedience by what he suffered"*
> (Hebrews 5:8, NCV).

This verifies that to have the character of God, to be the "express image" of Him, Jesus had to suffer, had to be *cut and sharpened* by choosing to obey His Father. Once again, if this applies to Christ, it applies to us if we are to be sons of God. We must choose to obey. We must take time to get to know God well enough to clearly hear Him so we can obey. We must be willing to suffer to have our habits formed to God's image.

EXPRESS IMAGE – MILITARY APPLICATION

This section was very exciting for me personally, as it totally changed my thinking – renewed my mind! Let's see if it does the same for you.

The second part of the definition of "express image" is the root of it all, identifying the battlefront, as it uses a military application - *a palisade or rampart, a mound for circumvallation in a siege.* Let's define those terms with Webster's 1828 and see what is revealed:

- Palisade – *a fence or fortification consisting of a row of stakes or posts (pales) sharpened and set firmly into the ground, 2-3 feet apart.*
- Rampart – *fortification; elevation or mound of ground capable of resisting cannon shot; that which fortifies and defends from assault and secures safety.*
- Circumvallation – *a wall or rampart surrounding the camp of a besieging army to prevent desertion* [their escape].

This series of definitions, and particularly circumvallation, created a totally opposite view of the battlefield from my previous under-standing. I had pictured my territory as the center of the battle, fighting the external

enemy, keeping him back or driving him away from my camp, keeping the enemy out and me safe within my walled fortress.

But, NO! The true meaning of circumvallation is keeping the <u>enemy confined</u> to a tiny camp and me FREE without boundaries.

This is a New Testament enemy, a spiritual enemy, an enemy inside my mind/thoughts that can be defeated, but never killed because you cannot kill a spirit. But as part of both myself and Jesus being the "express image" of God's person/nature, I was made to continually keep the enemy at bay, confined, unable to escape his camp or penetrate mine. The battlefield is inside: my mind, my heart. As my character continues to form (from *estimated character* of what I can acquire to *real character*, more like God's *exact image*), I will not only achieve further personal victories, but by keeping the enemy confined, I can expose him to others and help them also walk in greater and greater victory: going and growing from *estimated* character to *real* character; going from glory to glory.

This understanding captures the enemy and keeps his territory tiny, captive and confined. It also allows me, the son of God, an ever-growing territory, an ever-growing knowledge, freedom, peace, joy, and riches. This is <u>glory</u>: openness, expanse, enlargement, brightness. This is beginning to show the world an "honorable representation of God." This is the essence of being the "express image" of God's person or nature.

APPLICATION – BUT HOW DO WE DO IT?

The Bible is full of many stories of the incredible and miraculous works that Christ did in his lifetime. It's easy for us to argue that this was Jesus and we aren't Him. How can we possibly hope or aspire to rise to the level of Christ as a *son of God*? Jesus assures His followers that this is indeed possible – "*I tell you the truth, whoever believes in me will do the same things that I do. Those who believe will do even greater things than these...*" (John 14:12, NCV).

The wonderful news of this passage is the absolute verification that our Father has fully equipped us to become *sons of God,* able to do even greater things than Jesus! How can that be? More wonderful news – "*...we have the mind of Christ*" (1 Corinthians 2:16, NCV). Okay, but what does that really mean and how are we to plug into that mind and use it?

These are the questions we'll address in the next chapter. As we saw from the military application of being created in God's express image, we are at war and the battlefield is in our mind. This is where we must begin to take dominion – "*...bringing every thought into captivity to the obedience of Christ*" (2 Corinthians 10:5, NKJV) - thus, freeing our minds for the glory of God and His thoughts. We cordially invite you to continue in your study as we venture into the science of your mind, discover how it lines up with God's word, and what marvels lie there!

CHAPTER SIX

THE BATTLEFIELD OF THE MIND – TAKING DOMINION!

"For the weapons of our warfare are not carnal but mighty in God for pulling down strongholds, casting down arguments and every high thing that exalts itself against the knowledge of God, bringing every thought into captivity to the obedience of Christ" (2 Corinthians 10:4-5, NKJV).

REVIEWING & REITERATING

Discovering that we are the sons of God is an awesome and exciting, yet at the same time intimidating and overwhelming thought. But the reality of being a son of God - and performing the accompanying responsibilities of governing this world as He would - fits perfectly into our other findings in previous chapters:

- If the kingdom of heaven is here on this earth now, it is simply logical that the sons of God are the ones who should be ruling and reigning. (Chapter Two – Luke 17:20-21)
- If planet earth is not about to end in utter destruction, it is the sons of God who can demonstrate and bring forth God's kingdom of peace and restoration. (Chapter Three – Matthew 24)
- If our true hope is to go from *glory to glory* - becoming an honorable representation of God - this will be the outcome as we grow up and become mature sons of God. (Chapter Four – 2 Corinthians 3:18)
- As a son of God, we are created in God's *express image*, which imparts to us both inborn character traits and potential character that can be developed to enable us to learn and walk out this *sonship* with power and authority. (Chapter Five – Hebrews 1:3; Romans 8:29-30)

It is this latter part of the character of a son of God – the potential habits that can be learned and practiced – that begins in the battlefield of our minds, and what we will explore next. Time to get out those spiritual "thinking caps" again!

ANCIENT HISTORY & THE BIBLE

It is very encouraging to Bible-believing Christians today as discoveries of ancient artifacts are proving the veracity of scripture. Archeologists have located the ruins of Jericho with proof that the walls really did fall down (as if they were absorbed by the earth), just as the Bible says. Others have literally walked out the path of Moses and the

Israelites after they left Egypt, finding all the landmarks mentioned in the Bible and even a "land bridge" under the Red Sea where they most likely crossed safely. Chariot wheels and war implements have also been found on the floor of the Red Sea at this location, backing up the story of the demise of Pharaoh's army as they tried to overtake the Israelites. Fascinating.

MODERN SCIENCE & THE BIBLE

Of even more importance to us today is the modern science that is discovering new information about the brain - how we *think* and what happens internally and externally as a result. Newer and more precise brain-scanning instruments are able to map the brain's electrical activity in detail, actually watching the brain think. Their new discoveries are validating scripture passages such as: *"For as he thinks in his heart, so is he...."* (Proverbs 23:7, KJV).

This biblically-stated idea, that our thoughts have a direct impact on our reality, has now been observed scientifically. Thought is a powerful and controlling factor in what we manifest and create in our lives. Everything begins as an idea which then takes on physical form: You're hungry so you go get something to eat. You're lonely, so you go out with some friends.

Brain scanning machines bring a new clarity to a passage I have personally struggled with for years - *"Now faith is the <u>substance</u> of things hoped for, the <u>evidence</u> of things not seen"* (Hebrews 11:1, KJV). Faith is thought. Hope is thought. They are not tangible or touchable. Yet scripture declares that they are *substance* – something you can touch, evidence you can see. This statement is basically declaring that things intangible – faith and hope – are tangible. How can that be?

Modern science to the rescue! Thoughts actually create neural pathways through your brain tissue – pathways that can actually be seen with modern medical instruments. Faith and hope are some of the thoughts that create these pathways. It is noteworthy that these pathways are in the non-conscious part which makes up 96-98 percent of your brain. Do you realize that this means the bulk of our lives are determined by our non-conscious brain – things we are not even aware of thinking?

Want to know what you believe, what you have faith in, what you hope for? Look at your life. What do you see? Whatever you find there is evidence of your beliefs. Your current life – your relationships, your health, your income, your lifestyle, where you live, where you work, where you play, what you do every day, all of it – is an accurate reading of the picture you've been holding in your non-conscious brain. Your life is largely your creation and the principle tool you have used to create it is your beliefs, your thoughts – just as scripture declares, *"For as he thinks in his heart, so is he.... (Proverbs 23:7, KJV)*

This is why thinking right thoughts, correcting wrong thoughts, and consciously studying, speaking out and filling our minds with God's words and His thoughts are so important. As we *hope* for the right things, as we study and meditate on who God says we are and what He says we can do, new thoughts will become planted in our non-conscious mind and we begin creating a new neural network or pattern within our brains that corresponds to these new "God" thoughts. You are creating the seed that is required to start attracting resources necessary to allow those hopes, thoughts and beliefs to unfold into a physical manifestation. On a spiritual and flesh level you will begin taking actions, speaking, living and attracting circumstances to bring about these new thoughts.

THE POWER OF THINKING

Let's look at a few passages of scripture that speak of thinking and the mind, and see the power that lies within our thoughts. For if we are supposed to do even greater things than Christ (John 14:12), then we *must* discover and learn more about this power. Once again, we'll define some terms and reason through what we see.

2 Corinthians 10:4-5 (NKJV)

> *"For the weapons of our warfare are not carnal but mighty in God for pulling down <u>strongholds</u>, casting down <u>arguments</u> and every high thing that exalts itself against the knowledge of God, bringing every thought into captivity to the obedience of Christ."*

This passage states that the weapons of our warfare are not carnal - not the traditional swords, cannons or other artillery. The weapons we are to use are mighty for pulling down a very different kind of *stronghold* which <u>Strong's Concordance</u> defines as –

- Stronghold – *fortify through the <u>idea</u> of holding safely*

These strongholds are *ideas*, not physical structures. The weapons we are to use are mighty for casting down arguments or *imaginations* – more words for thoughts and ideas. <u>Webster's 1828</u> definition is very revealing and explains how our wrong thoughts can create obstacles that are very hard to overcome –

- Imaginations – *The power or faculty of the mind by which it conceives and forms ideas of things communicated to it by the organs of sense. It selects the parts of different conceptions or objects of memory to form a whole <u>more</u> pleasing, <u>more</u> terrible, <u>more</u> awful than has ever been presented in the ordinary course of nature.*

Thinking through these two definitions, let's review: God's weapons will pull down strongholds – the place (my thoughts) where my wrong ideas, my wrong imaginations have been fortified and held "safely," where they could not be challenged by the right ideas from God's word. These are the places (arguments) where I have consciously (or non-consciously) convinced myself of lies that keep me from controlling myself or stopping wrong actions, or not performing right ones. These false conclusions have come about through the *power of my mind* of things communicated to it through my senses – my flesh. My memory even *magnifies* these wrong ideas/lies, making them *more* pleasing, *more* terrible, *more* awful than they really are or ever could be, fortifying the lie in my mind.

God tells me to walk by faith, not sight, not by my five senses. I am to use His Word and Spirit and my spirit to come to truth. I am to cast down any and all imaginations that *exalt themselves* over Him and His truth. I am to replace these lies by taking *captive* the true thoughts. A captive is locked or confined in a place. If my mind is a place where God's thoughts are held captive as this verse declares, then there is *no escape of right thinking.* The wrong thoughts cannot occupy the same space. They must leave, or at least be cast down, overpowered, overcome by truth. This is a description of warfare over a piece of turf – a thought. Winning such a battle, striking down a lie and raising up the truth, will result in a visible victory in our lives. Changed thoughts equal changed actions.

There are many such thought battlefields where we struggle between what we think and what God's word actually says. For example, if God's word says I will do greater things than Christ (John 14:12), then I will do greater things than Christ, no matter how impossible that may sound. If God says I am a priest and a king (1 Peter 2:9), then I am and I have the authority and power that accompanies those positions, even if I don't "feel" like anybody listens to me. If God says I can be a partaker of His divine nature (2 Peter 1:4), then I am able to do so, as amazing as that statement is along with all the implications. These statements are a far cry from what many churches teach about being "just a sinner saved by grace." God has a much higher view of His sons than this!

We need to change our thinking and agree with who God says we are and what we are capable of doing. Most of us have allowed our minds to be filled with wrong thoughts for so long that they have become "strongholds" that need to be taken down. But, we can and we must cast down those erroneous arguments, create new thoughts, new imaginations that are captive and obedient to Christ and what God's word says. This brings us to the next verse:

<u>Romans 12:2 (NKJV)</u>

"Do not be <u>conformed</u> to this world, but be <u>transformed</u> by the renewing of your mind, that you may prove what is the good and acceptable and perfect will of God."

As is our custom, let's define some terms from <u>Webster's 1828</u>, then think through what we find.

- Conform – *to comply with or yield; to live or act according to* [this world].
- Transform – *In theology to change the natural disposition and temper of man from a state of enmity to God and his law, into the image of God, or into a disposition and temper conformed to the will of God.*

It is very noteworthy that this word *transform,* in <u>Strong's Concordance</u>, is the same one used for the *transfiguration* of Christ on a mountaintop before the eyes of Peter, James and John, when *"His face shone like the sun and His clothes became as white as the light"* (Matthew 17:2, NKJV), and he visibly and audibly communicated with Moses, Elijah and his heavenly Father. This is another picture of what we – the sons of God – are to be able to do. Wow. To even begin to grasp such things we do, indeed, need to *renew our minds.*

In addition, look at what the result is when we do renew our minds – We will *"prove what is the good and acceptable and perfect will of God."* The word *prove* actually means to discern or examine. In other words, a transformed, renewed mind will be able to discern and examine God's will. Wouldn't it be great to have this ability? How often do we struggle, search and desire to know God's will in any particular situation? Here's how you find it. Be transformed. Renew your mind. And be encouraged, for this is very possible as evidenced by the next verse:

1 Corinthians 2:16 (NKJV)

"...But we have the <u>mind</u> of Christ."

<u>Strong's Concordance</u> gives a profound definition of *mind,* which leads us to two equally mind-boggling follow-up definitions from <u>Webster's 1828</u> –

- Mind – *<u>divine</u> or human <u>intellect</u>*
- Divine - *godlike*
- Intellect – *the faculty of thinking; otherwise called understanding.*

APPLYING THESE VERSES

As we review, I pray God will help you to begin to renew your mind and spirit and bring them into obedience to His Word, His plan for you. Like Paul encouraged the Philippians – *"...there is one thing I always do. Forgetting the past and straining toward what is ahead...the goal...for which God called me..."* (Philippians 3:13-14, NCV). You cannot change the past - *forget it* - as Paul says. But you most certainly can shape your present and future - *strain towards the goal for which God has called you!* As you renew your mind, you will be coming alive to excitement, purpose and rewards you can scarcely imagine at this point. These are the things we need to begin imagining!

I will write this paragraph in first person and describe how I have gone (and continue to go) through this mind renewal process. I came to realize I have accepted, magnified and meditated upon negative thoughts of myself in my mind and created my own personal stronghold. God, forgive me. This self-exaltation of self-abasement (seeming contradiction in terms) sets my thoughts above who God says I am. I needed to renew my mind. It is what God thinks that counts. I am what He says I am. I can do what He says I can do. I can be who He says I can be. To make excuses, believe less, be less or do less is to be outside His will and not fulfilling my God-ordained purpose. I prayed and asked God to help me begin to build new places in my mind, new thoughts to be held captive. To say "I can't because..." or "I don't deserve it" is to *exalt myself above the knowledge of God.* God forbid! It was time to find God's thoughts and make them my imaginings.

BEGIN TO CHANGE YOUR THINKING!

Take every thought captive to the obedience of Christ. Why? Because our thoughts determine our life's outcomes. Cast down every imagination that exalts itself above God. Why? Because imagination is thought and thoughts usher in reality. God knew our thoughts - whether resident in the conscious or non-conscious part of our brains - determine our actions which determine our outcomes in life, for good or evil.

Wrong thoughts have bad consequences. Worry, regret and fear are thoughts of what you don't want. Job was consumed with worry over his children's behavior. He prayed and made burned offerings for fear that his children may have sinned and cursed God in their hearts.

When absolute tragedy struck and all his children were killed in one day, he said, *"For the thing which I greatly feared is come upon me and that which I was afraid of is come to me"* (Job 3:25, KJV).

You have far more capacity to create the events and circumstances in your life than you have ever imagined possible! This is part of God's design and the way He created you. Imagination is the seat of your capacity to create. When you think the same thing over and over, it eventually becomes a habit of thought. A habit of thought over time and with repetition becomes an attitude or belief. These beliefs and habits are profoundly stronger than our desires and often become self-fulfilling prophecy, for good or evil.

Now take a test. When you read the underlined sentence in the previous paragraph telling you of your capacity to create events and circumstances in your life, what was your reaction? What was your first thought? Did you think – "She doesn't know what I'm up against."? Or, "She doesn't have to live with my family."? Or, "She has no idea what I have to put up with at work."? If these or any negative thoughts like them were the first to enter your mind, you have a stronghold that needs to be taken down. You need to take such thoughts captive and turn them around to reflect the reality of who God declares you are and what He says about you.

Remember, you have the mind of Christ. By definition this means you have a *godlike ability to think and understand*. Remember, you can be a partaker of God's divine nature (2 Peter 1:4). You are a saint (Ephesians 1:1). Find out what that means and start thinking and acting like one. You are a priest and a king (1 Peter 2:9) – someone who cares for the things of God and rules with Him. Study and meditate on these verses and ask God to show you some applications in your life, and then do them. You can receive grace and mercy to help you whenever you need it (Hebrews 4:16). Take God up on that promise by turning your thinking around to receive it.

A MODERN DAY PARABLE

Jesus taught through the use of parables – regular, every-day stories from which a moral or instruction could be drawn. Let's look at a modern-day parable on new thoughts:

One day a man decided to go on a hike through a stretch of wild forest, a tract that had never been traveled before. He had to knock tree limbs out of the way, treading on overgrown plants and grasses underfoot. In some places, he tripped and fell due to the difficulty of the terrain. As he retraced his steps on the way back later that day, he could just barely make out the path he had traveled a few hours earlier: a broken limb here, a bit of flattened grasses there.

The next day he came back to the same stretch of forest and he made the trek again, following the same path, but this time the trail he had blazed the day before was slightly easier to follow. He didn't trip and fall even once as most of the limbs, plants and grasses were no longer the obstacles they had been. Day after day he repeated this journey, widening the trail, compressing the grass and eventually he had created an obvious, comfortable pathway through the forest. What had been difficult and nearly impassable was now a pleasant and familiar stroll.[7]

End of parable. Beginning of explanation - What does a hike in uncharted woods have to do with thinking? This story is a great illustration of the incredible truth of what happens when we start to renew our minds – to create new neural pathways. It may take an incredible act of will and imagination to have a new thought, to forge that new pathway in your brain. It can take a similar leap of faith, courage and imagination to picture yourself as God sees you. You're cutting a new path through thickets of habitual thoughts which can be one stubborn, overgrown forest indeed. But you make the leap and slice through the underbrush with your new thought, and in the process, you start laying down a new trail.

Scientifically speaking, we are actually and literally reprogramming what is known as the reticular activating system and recalibrating your psycho-cybernetic mechanism. You are overriding your genetic programming and your upbringing with all its years of ingrained habit. This is no small task!

In laymen's terms, here is what is happening inside your brain: Neurologically, your thought is carried along a series of electrical impulses, moving from neuron to neuron by leaping across the gaps, or synapses, in between. For that thought's electrical charge to leap the synaptic chasm, a certain electrical threshold must be reached and exceeded. And with that leap, something fascinating happens. You begin ever so slightly to lower that threshold. The next time you evoke that same thought, there is a tiny bit less electrical resistance to that same synaptic leap. Over time, as you repeat the thought over and over (meditating!), the threshold gets lower and lower, making it easier and easier to pass along those electrical charges, easier to have the thought. You are bushwhacking a new pathway with your thoughts.

"Neuroscientists have an expression: 'Neurons that fire together wire together.' As your new thought pattern is repeated over and over, the new neural patterns in your brain literally wire themselves together, creating a brand-new network of neurons. In time, your new path becomes a superhighway, across which the constant traffic of your new beliefs and new identify drive effortlessly and automatically."[8] Changing from the inside out, you have paved the way for your new self as a mature son of God!

A FRESH START

Begin anew. Start today. Pray and ask God to help you immediately identify wrong thoughts as they occur, and then take that thought captive to the obedience of Christ by speaking out loud the truth of what God says on the subject. Crises and suffering can be opportunities for accelerated spiritual growth and a chance to gain more knowledge of the word of God and what He has to say about you and your circumstances. Do not allow opposing thoughts! Take dominion over your thought life! Start to deal with your wrong thinking in a new way. Begin to _meditate_ on specific scripture passages.

- Meditate – *to dwell on anything in thought; to contemplate; to study; to turn or revolve any subject in the mind.*

For example - Thoughts of helplessness are not from God. Reject them. Replace them with God's word:

"I can do all things through Christ who strengthens me" (Philippians 4:13, NKJV).

Thoughts of despair and regret over the past are not from God. Reject them. Replace them with God's word:

"...whatever things are noble...just...pure... lovely...good report...praiseworthy – meditate on these things" (Philippians 4:8, NKJV).

WRITE IT DOWN!

Write helpful scripture verses on sticky notes and put them in places where you will constantly see them – on your bathroom mirror, your car dashboard, the refrigerator, your cubicle wall or desk at work. Every time your eyes fall upon these sticky notes, meditate on these passages – dwell on them, turn them over in your mind. Read the verse out loud. Ask yourself questions. What does this verse mean to you personally right now in the situation you find yourself? How would you feel if you do it? What would it look like? What actions would you take? What would be the first step? Picture in your mind walking out and working out a solution according to God's thoughts.

Most importantly, get a blank notebook (or a beautiful journal!) and make time to begin writing out these new thoughts and revelations that are the product of your prayers and meditations. These revelations are coming from your heavenly Father and will be personal and powerful. You can read them over and over to continue to build that new superhighway of right thinking in your brain. Use the method we've used in these pamphlets of defining various terms within your scriptures passages, and then write out the applications. This journal will be a most valuable vehicle on your journey of repair and restoration of your heart and mind.

The best news in all of this mind renewal is the fact that it is not just an act of your will power that will bring this to pass. You will not be working alone.

DISCOVERING YOUR PURPOSE & YOUR POWER

God will be working with you. As you continue through this renewing of the mind process – taking the wrong thoughts captive and replacing them and meditating on what God says about you – you will begin to discover your role as a son of God. You will begin seeing things through the mind of Christ that He gave to you.

You were created for a purpose. God chose his Son to *"own all things"* (Hebrews 1:2) and *"to hold it all together"* (Hebrews 1:3). As sons of God we are *"joint heirs with Christ"* (Romans 8:16-17); therefore, we share both this inheritance and the accompanying responsibility. What a purpose! What a partnership! And look at some of the promises God gives you of empowerment to do it:

> *"...as many as received him, to them he gave <u>power</u> to become the sons of God, even to them that believe on his name"* (John 1:12, KJV).

> *"...that you may know...what is the exceeding greatness of His <u>power</u> toward us who believe..."* (Ephesians 1:18-19, NKJV).

"For God has not given us a spirit of fear, but of <u>power</u> and of love and of a sound mind" (2 Timothy 1:7, NKJV).

It is imperative we understand more about our purpose and the power that accompanies it. What exactly does it mean to *"own all things"* and *"hold it all together"*? As a son of God, how much power and authority do you actually have? Over whom do you have this power and authority? How are you to exercise it? How will it manifest? And how does it relate to *"holding it all together"*? These are questions we'll tackle in the next chapter.

CHAPTER SEVEN

THE PURPOSE & POWER OF THE SONS OF GOD

"...God has chosen his Son to <u>own all things</u>... The Son reflects the glory of God and shows exactly what God is like. He [the Son] *<u>holds everything together</u> with his <u>powerful word</u>..."* (Hebrews 1:2-3, NCV).

CONTINUING THE JOURNEY

In our previous chapter we used a parable of walking through a wild forest, blazing a completely new trail as we renew our minds to discover, embrace and apply the truth of what God says about us. The truths we are uncovering, however, are not really new. They've been in God's word all along. But they are new to us as we uncover a deeper understanding of them and actually begin to put them into practice.

In this chapter, we will study our purpose, our inheritance and the power that accompanies it. WARNING LABEL: This is going to be particularly mind-stretching.

My prayer is that each of you will take your time - ponder and meditate on these powerful truths - and let the words impart their truth to your heart. The chorus of a song called "Ancient Words" puts it well:

Ancient words, ever true.
Changing me and changing you.
We have come with open hearts.
Oh, let the ancient words impart.

REVIEWING AGAIN!

At the risk of seeming too redundant, I want to again summarize where we've been so as to clarify where we're going. It is a step-by-step process to become a mature son of God, to go from *glory to glory.* We are to grow in our understanding and application of God's word and His plan for us and this world. It is my hope that these chapters are leading you on such a journey.

- Chapter Two – The kingdom of heaven is a present reality, not a future event. It is here now because it is *within* believers. (Luke 17:20-21)
- Chapter Three – The "end of the world" Jesus spoke of was actually the "end of an age" and not the end of planet earth. (Matthew 24)
- Chapter Four – Our greatest hope in this life is not to escape it, but to become an ever-improving and "honorable representation of God." (2 Corinthians 3:18)
- Chapter Five – Sons of God have both inborn and potential character traits. When these are working together we are increasingly enabled to walk out our

sonship with power and authority. (Hebrews 1:3; Romans 8:29-30)

- Chapter Six – Changing our thinking – renewing our minds – is the primary battlefield in realizing and living out this *sonship.* (2 Corinthians 10:4-5)

As we progress in our understanding of who we are (sons of God – John 1:12), our *purpose* or what we are called to do (rule and reign as kings and priests – 1 Peter 2:9), it is becoming increasingly clear that we will need tremendous *power* to accomplish these feats. Letting scripture be our guide once again, let's reason through how this works.

YOUR PURPOSE - LET THE ANCIENT WORDS IMPART

Hebrews 1:2-3 is a beautiful description of God's plans for His Son, the purpose for which He sent him into this world, and the power with which He equipped him. We'll look at three key parts:

- God chose His Son to *"own all things"* (Hebrews 1:2).
- The Son *"holds everything together"* (Hebrews 1:3).
- He does this with *"his powerful word"* (Hebrews 1:3).

The Son Owns All Things – Hebrews 1:2

The Son owns all things because his Father God chose to give all things to him. This is an inheritance. Jesus is the designated heir. Check out the incredible parallel truth to this passage: *"The Spirit Himself bears witness... that we are* [sons] *of God...heirs of God and joint heirs with*

Christ..." (Romans 8:16-17, NKJV). Clearly, what God has given to His Son (his inheritance – *all things*) also belongs to us (if we are sons of God).

What is it we have inherited with Christ? All things. What does this mean? Can we really take this literally? The word *all* is a term without boundaries – physical or spiritual. But how do we begin to define "all things?" The Apostle Paul mentions a few specifics when speaking to both the Corinthian and Ephesian believers: *"...All things belong to you...the world, life, death, the present and the future – all these belong to you"* (1 Corinthians 3:21-22, NCV).

> *"God... put* [Christ] *at his right side in the heavenly world...over all rulers, authorities, powers and kings, not only in this world but also in the next. God put everything under his power..."* (Ephesians 1:20-22, NCV).

Both of these passages refer to an inheritance in the physical and spiritual realm, the tangible and intangible. The latter passage also states that, *"God put everything under his power."* This means that Jesus not only owns everything, he has also been given power over everything he owns, which means he is to rule or govern it. Christ's position at God's *right side* (or hand) is acknowledged by Biblical scholars as referring to the seat of power and authority. Okay, that's Jesus, but what about us? We may be joint heirs of *all things,* but how could we possibly have equal power? This same passage of Ephesians addresses that very subject:

> *"I pray also that you will have greater under-standing in your heart so you will know... that <u>God's power is very great for us</u> who believe"* (Ephesians 1:18-19, NCV).

> *"[God] <u>raised us up with Christ</u> and gave us a <u>seat with him</u> in the heavens"* (Ephesians 2:6, NCV).

Amazingly and clearly, this passage declares that God's power *for us* is very great, and then clarifies and quanti-fies it further by saying He has put us in that same seat of power with Christ: at his right hand, *a seat with Jesus in the heavens.* This bends my mind and makes me think I am being blasphemous, but I didn't say it. God's word declared it: sons of God; joint heirs; a seat with Jesus in the heavens; over all rulers, authorities, powers and kings, in this world and the next! How can this be? How can we grasp this? How can we do this? Let's move on to the next passage as we look for these answers.

<u>The Son *"Holds Everything Together"*</u> – Hebrews 1:3

The King James Bible renders this phrase *upholding all things*. <u>Strong's Concordance </u>gives several short definitions:

* Upholding – *bear or carry; bring forth; enduring; go on; lead; move.*

These definitions confirm that God's intention in giving *all things* to Jesus was that he would also bear or carry the responsibility for *all things*. He would endure whatever he had to endure. He would go on, not quit. He would lead. These are governmental terms. This is the fulfillment of Isaiah's prophecy: *"For to us a Child is born...and the gov-ernment shall be upon His shoulder..."* (Isaiah 9:6, NKJV). Strong's Concordance gives a very thought provoking defi-nition of government that fits perfectly into Christ's role as royalty:

- Government – [from #8280] – *prevail; have power as a prince.*
- Government – *direct, control, regulate, restrain* (Webster's 1828)

The Webster's 1828 definition of government uses words that convey the same meaning as *upholding.* In other words, the inheritance that Jesus received (and we also as joint heirs) is not just the earth and all that is in it. It is *all* the responsibility that goes with *upholding* it: gov-erning, directing, restraining, leading, ruling and reigning. It is taking dominion over all the earth as Adam was com-manded to do in the garden (Genesis 1:28). Also of tremen-dous importance – the Strong's Concordance definition is to *prevail.* In other words, Christ's government *wins.* The words *carry, endure, lead* all indicate hard work, but the word *prevail* indicates ultimate victory! This is great encouragement for those times when we are battle weary.

THE GREAT COMMISSION INCLUDES WHAT!?!

Now, let's take a fresh look at Christ's Great Commission as it relates to all of this, connecting it to the sons of God *holding all things together* by directing and leading prop-erly. Think for a moment of the myriad of applications in the world in which we live. By and large, the church has reduced its message and purpose to saving people from hell so they can go to heaven when they die. A few churches occasionally have an outreach program or two. The reality is so much bigger. Read the Great Commission passage with fresh eyes and see the larger meaning:

> *"All power in heaven and on earth is given to me. So go and make followers of all people in the world. Baptize them...and teach them to obey everything that I have taught you..."* (Matthew 28:18-20, NCV).

This is a two-fold commission: an evangelistic mandate - *baptizing people*, AND a cultural mandate - *teaching them to obey everything* Jesus taught. As stated above, most Christian churches have embraced the evangelistic duty or purpose of leading people to salvation through Christ. But what of the cultural command? Christianity begins as a personal relationship with Christ, but it doesn't end there. You have a purpose that extends into serving the world in one capacity or another. What are we teaching those newborn babes in Christ about how to walk out their new life in their every day life of family, work, or school? Are we *teaching them to obey everything* Jesus taught in these spheres?

Jesus taught on government and politics, education, taxation, marriage and family, employer-employee relationships, honest wages, free-market bargaining, private property rights, proper use of finances, dangers of debt, penal restraints upon criminals, lawsuits... just to name a few. He literally covered every area of life!

Tragically, most of the church today has ignored the cultural mandate entirely. They have left politics, law, economics, education and other social issues to the ungodly, declaring such things to be in the realm of the physical world. Surely, they say, Christians should be involved in spiritual issues and not become entangled in the affairs of the world.

Thankfully, defining our terms will once again shine a bright light on truth. Look at <u>Webster's 1828</u> definition of politics:

- Politics – *the science of government; that <u>part of ethics</u> which consists in the regulation and government of a nation or state for the preservation of its safety peace and prosperity…also for the protection of its citizens in their rights, with the <u>preservation and improvement of their morals</u>.*

Who is better equipped to teach about *ethics* and the *preservation and improvement of morals* – Christians or non-Christians? Who did Jesus command to *teach obedience to everything* He taught? It wasn't the unbelievers! And it is also not just *children* of God, but more specifically, it should be the mature *sons of God.* The political and cultural mess we are in today stems largely from the absence of mature, wise Christian involvement. All too often Christians have abdicated their responsibility of leadership in the every day moments of life – the cultural mandate.

The sons of God should be spreading truth, liberty, justice, and prosperity among the nations by instructing all individuals in the Biblical principles of every area of life. Such education would benefit every culture on earth.

One of the most emotionally-charged scriptures declares that the world - all of creation - is earnestly waiting for the sons of God to be revealed: *"For the earnest expectation of the creature waiteth for the manifestation of the sons of God"* (Romans 8:19 – KJV).

- Earnest – *shrieking; crying out, groaning* (Strong's Concordance)
- Manifestation – *disclosure; appearing; coming; revelation* (Strong's Concordance)

This is more than dramatic. Creation is literally *shrieking, crying out, and groaning* while waiting for the sons of God to show up and do their duty. The New Century version rendering of this passage adds even more clarity and passion: *"Everything God made is waiting with excitement for God to show his children's glory completely"* (Romans 8:19, NCV). Remember the definition of glory?

- Glory – *honorable representation of God.*

THINK OF THE POSSIBILITIES!

So, all of creation is eagerly waiting for the sons of God, those who can be an *honorable representation of God,* to show themselves. How will that happen? How will they be recognized? The applications are as varied as the opportunities. Think of the areas that would be impacted:

- Those who influence knowledge – pastors, teachers, doctors, scientists, engineers, journalists, media of all sorts.

- Those who influence money – businessmen, bankers, entrepreneurs, real estate developers.
- Those who influence law – government leaders, judges, lawyers, political activists, law enforcement officers.

God has given each of us gifts, abilities and passions. We can be sure there are Christians employed or involved in every one of the above-mentioned areas. I believe some of them are already beginning to manifest their role as sons of God, perhaps unknowingly. Their ethics, their creativity, their integrity have impacted those around them. Imagine the effect on the world as more and more Christians begin to understand what it means to be a son of God, walking in obedience and taking dominion. Imagine the gradual transformation as they begin teaching, leading by example, and connecting leaders of education, business and politics to *transform their culture for Christ* – not just saving sinners. It is their inheritance. It is their purpose. The sons of God are to be directing *all things in this world*.

YOUR POWER - LET THE ANCIENT WORDS IMPART

But this is not just a battle of the flesh. Our dominion is not just to be exercised in the physical world. The battle begins in the spirit. And thank God, our dominion extends into the spiritual realm as well: *"God... put* [Christ] *...over all rulers, authorities, powers and kings, not only in this world but also in the next ..."* (Ephesians 1:20-22, NCV).

How in the world does God think we are up to such tasks, either physical through cultural transformation, or spiritual rulership? He tells us with the next phrase of our Hebrews passage. It's all about power. Let's have a look.

He Does This With *"His Powerful Word"* - Hebrews 1:3

Now that we have discerned *what* our inheritance is (all things), and the *purpose* intended for the sons of God is to rule over all things, we need to learn *how* we are to do it. We most certainly cannot do it on our own. How are we to rule, uphold, *govern* over all these things that we have inherited as sons of God? This passage declares that Jesus does it with *his powerful word,* and since we are to emulate Jesus, so should we. To do so, we need to find out what this *powerful word* is. We'll begin by defining what *word* this is referring to.

Strong's Concordance lists only two Greek words for *word.* For better understanding we'll define both so we can compare the two. The first one - *logos* - is *not* used in this Hebrews passage. The second – *rhema* - is the word used in the Hebrews passage:

- Word – *logos* – *something said; thought; reasoning; preaching*
- Word – *rhema* – *narration or command*

Let's think through these two meanings. Though these are both powerful, *logos* can be spoken or simply thought or reasoned through – your private meditations. It's what I hope each of you are doing as you read each of these volumes. *Rhema,* on the other hand, is always spoken and it is done either as narration (teaching by <u>one</u>), or *command* – an obvious reflection of exercising authority and power over others.

A command is demanding by nature and an obvious method of ruling and governing. This type of *word* would be most appropriate in matters of law: with government leaders, judges, lawyers, political activists, or law enforcement officers. However, it is probably not the most useful tool for swaying or influencing people in other areas of the culture, such as education and business. A commanding person in these arenas is an overbearing person. As we study the life of Jesus, the situations in which he used commanding language was most often in dealing with rooting out evil spirits, not demanding people obey God.

But what about *narration?* Narration could be preaching or teaching individuals or groups. It can also be story-telling. This allows people to think and reason through what is being said. According to this Hebrews passage, this is the way Jesus ruled over all things – by either commanding or narrating. We need discernment to determine which type of *word* would be appropriate in which situations.

Some of Jesus' most powerful words were spoken in parables, a form of narration. The Pharisees were furious at the telling of the story of the Vinedresser (Matthew 21:33-45) because they understood Jesus was referring to their loss of the kingdom of heaven due to their evil ways. Stories can be more convicting than pointing an accusing finger. This is because we are to tell these stories, speak these truths, with God's *power.* Here again, there are several Greek words for power and it is very enlightening to learn them all for better clarification of the term used in Hebrews 1:3.

WHAT KIND OF POWER?

For those of you who are into statistics, I counted 152 uses of the word *power* in <u>Strong's Concordance</u> (in the

New Testament), with seven different meanings. Eighteen of them are of the first five connotations, which we'll cover below, but the remaining 134 will be on the last two applications which will be where we spend most of our study time.

The first five are -

- *Power of governing authorities or magistrates (#746 – Luke 20:20)*
- *Heavenly power of angels which is greater than the power of evil man (#2479 – 2 Peter 2:11; 2 Thessalonians 1:9)*
- *Delegated or borrowed power – the beast was given power (for a specific task) (#1325 – Revelation 13:14-15)*
- *Vigor, dominion, strength – "...honor and power belong to God..." (#2904 – 1 Timothy 6:16); "...according to his glorious power..." (Colossians 1:11)*
- *Majestic, magnificent power – amazement at the mighty power of God...Jesus casting out a spirit of epilepsy (#3168 – Luke 9:43)*

As stated above, these five kinds of power are seen in eighteen places, but by far there are two words for power that overwhelmingly predominate these others, being used 134 times! The second most often used word for power (62 times) is #1849 –

- Power – *[Greek – exousia] - ability, privilege, capacity, freedom, control, delegated influence; jurisdiction, right [to exercise your authority upon]* –

Examples:

> *"...all power in heaven and on earth..." (Great Commission)* (Matthew 28:18)

> *[Spiritual] power over the enemy* (Luke 10:19)

> *Pilate had power to crucify or release Jesus* (John 19:10).

> *"...power to become sons of God..."* (John 1:12)

But, the <u>most used</u> word for power (72 times) is the word in Hebrews 1:3 - #1411 –

- Power – *[Greek – dunamis]* – <u>*miraculous*</u> *power*

Examples:

> *"...the kingdom of God come[s] with power..."* (Mark 9:1)

> *"...Yours is the kingdom and the power..."* (Matthew 6:13)

> *"...shall receive power when the Holy Spirit has come upon you..."* (Acts 1:8)

> *God has given us a spirit of power* (2 Timothy 1:7).

- Miraculous - *performed supernaturally by a power beyond the ordinary agency of natural laws; effected by the direct agency of Almighty power and not by natural causes.* (Webster's 1828)

THE INCREDIBLE APPLICATIONS

These two words for power are very different in their application and manifestation, so I would like to address each of them separately.

POWER – EXOUSIA

For purposes of brevity, we'll just look at two application of this type of power, though this is a very worthy topic upon which to spend some serious personal study and meditation time.

First, let's examine John 1:12 - the fact that you have the *power to become* a son of God. You have the *privilege* and *capacity.* But, it is not required. While our heavenly Father wants what is best for you (and for this world), He will not <u>force</u> you to make those decisions. God's power does not extinguish our freedom of choice; i.e. salvation is free and God wants everyone to have it, but He will not compel us to accept it. The same is true for becoming a son of God. It is God's desire for you and the best gift He can give you. It is a *privilege* and you have the *capacity.* But it is your choice to receive it or not. But please remember – all creation is waiting – *shrieking, crying out and groaning* – for <u>you</u> to grow up and use this power as a son of God!

Second, this power – *ability or delegated influence* – is what was conveyed to believers in the Great Commission. You have been given the *right to exercise your God-given authority* over *all things*. Let's look at an example of this in just one realm – law making and our federal government.

The United States was founded under God, and the Declaration of Independence declares *the laws of nature and nature's God* to be the basis for all law in America. Defining this phrase reveals that it includes the original <u>written</u> law - the Ten Commandments (*laws of nature's God)* - and the <u>unwritten</u> law - your God-created conscience (*the laws of nature).* Because you were created in the image and likeness of God, your God-created conscience lets you know instinctively that some things are plainly wrong - like killing a child. This is an example of a *law of nature.* Such laws do not need to be written down.

Here is the huge take-home point - <u>Any law that is contrary to *the laws of nature and nature's God* is not a legitimate law.</u>

But look where we find ourselves in this nation today in regard to this simple truth regarding the killing of a child. Abortion has been declared "legal" in all circumstances at any time. How can this be? For it most certainly violates both the <u>written</u> law – Thou shall not kill – and the <u>unwritten</u> law of your conscience. The truth remains intact: Killing a child at any age is an unlawful act - indeed, a monstrous, wicked, evil crime against an innocent baby who cannot defend itself.

But, because we have elected individuals to represent us who are <u>not sons of God</u>, the powerful word of truth - *rhema* - has not been spoken into this situation. Or more accurately, when *rhema* has been spoken it has not been backed up sufficiently with law-making/legislative action by *we the people* of America. We have allowed the ungodly to rule in our place and <u>50 million babies</u> have been killed as a result! This is unfathomable, yet it is true. We have the power to stop abortion, but we have not used it. In addition, simply speaking *rhema* into a situation does not mean it will always be received and acted upon. But this *power* includes the *right to exercise authority*. So, if speaking is not enough, we have the *right* to take action, to insist on legislation to protect life, not take it.

This is just one appalling and tragic example of why all of creation is *shrieking, crying out, and groaning* while waiting for the sons of God to show up and perform their God-ordained duties. (Romans 8:19) God did not intend for those who do not believe in Him to be running this planet. He wants us to be in charge and rule, if we have the true knowledge of the true God. Though we are not assured of the results, we are to use our *exousia power* as an act of obedience, regardless of the outcome. One of my favorite Founding Fathers, John Quincy Adams, said it well: *"Duty is ours. Results are God's."*

POWER – DUNAMIS

Next, let's look at the most sacred of all power - *dunamis*. Fasten your seat belt and open your mind and heart as we enter here, for we are headed for holy ground.

[DISCLAIMER: As I try to put this next section into words I feel woefully inadequate to explain this incredible power, and I reserve the "right to be wrong." The more I learn, the less I realize I know! Nevertheless, I will provide my thoughts and understanding as best I can, laying a foundation from which I hope you will study and build your own understanding.]

While *exousia power* endues us with the authority to act in any given situation, we cannot always be sure of the results. *Dunamis power*, on the other hand, is not something *delegated* to us that we can choose to use or not. It is not an *ability* that has been given us. Rather, *dunamis power* belongs to God alone, but if our hearts and minds are in the right place – in unity with our heavenly Father in any given set of circumstances – then this *dunamis power* flows through us to meet a need supernaturally.

In scripture, *dunamis power* is always connected directly to God, to the kingdom of God, or to the sons of God. Therefore, it is always a demonstration of God's will, for both individuals and for the earth. It is a power so strong it can actually <u>overrule</u> natural law – such as Jesus speaking to a violent storm and telling it to stop – and it did (Mark 4:37-39); or Christ walking on water and inviting Peter to do the same (Matthew 14:25-29). This is also the power God gave the apostles at Pentecost (Acts 1:8). We're going to look more closely at this particular passage as it is helpful in understanding more of the nature of this power - *"But you shall receive power when the Holy Spirit has <u>come</u> upon you..."* (Acts 1:8, NKJV)

Here is a common word – *come* – used nearly 600 times in the New Testament. And yet, this particular Greek word for *come* in the Acts 1:8 passage - *eperchomai* - is only used seven times, and has a very distinct and different meaning. Follow the amazing progression:

- Come [upon] – *to <u>supervene</u>; from #1909 – <u>superimposition</u> of time, place, order, etc.* (<u>Strong's Concordance</u>)
- Supervene – *to come upon as something <u>extraneous</u>* (<u>Webster's 1828</u>)

- Extraneous – *not belonging to a thing* (Webster's 1828)
- Superimposition – *act of laying or state of being placed on something else* (Webster's 1828)

Let's think this through in relation to the *dunamis power* of the Holy Spirit coming upon the disciples at Pentecost - the very first manifestation of such *power* coming upon man - and the same *power* God gives to all believers: *"For God has not given us a <u>spirit</u> of fear, but of <u>power</u> and of love and of a sound mind"* (2 Timothy 1:7, NKJV).

Using the definitions we can discern that this *Spirit of power* comes <u>upon</u> something to which it does not belong. It is God's Spirit and power, not ours. Though God *gives* us this power, it is temporarily superimposed upon us, but is not part of us. It is His power flowing through us *when it comes upon us.* God never leaves us (Hebrews 13:5). He is an ever-present reality in our lives. But, His *dunamis power* is not always in use in us, but only *comes upon* us in specific times and places as He ordains. It is His power and He uses it *through* the sons of God.

Once again, Jesus as the first-born Son of God, is our example to see how God's *dunamis power* was manifested in his life: *"…The Lord was giving Jesus the power to heal people"* (Luke 5:17, NCV). This corroborates the understanding that the power present for Jesus to heal was given to him by God. The power did not belong to Jesus. Jesus openly declared the acts he performed were not done under his power: *"But if I with the finger of God cast out devils, no doubt the kingdom of God is come upon you"* (Luke 11:20, KJV). Jesus cast out the devil, but he did so with *the finger of God.* Jesus used the power, but the power came from God.

To better comprehend this we could use the analogy of electric power. Electricity flows through a cord to send power to a designated place, a light bulb in a lamp, for example. The cord has no power of its own, but it carries the power to where it is needed. In addition, the cord needs to be plugged into the source of power in order to transfer it.

Consider the story of the woman with the issue of blood (Mark 5:25-34). She placed her faith in touching the hem of Jesus' garment in order to be healed. When she did so, it was in the midst of a large crowd of people. The passage declares that people were pressing in on Jesus on every side, yet he knew when she had touched his cloak. How? Because he said he felt *power* go out of him. This passage is particularly thought-provoking in that Jesus' mind/thoughts were not even involved in this healing. He didn't even know this woman was there, much less what her needs were. Jesus was the conduit – the vessel – through which God's power flowed for this woman's healing. This miracle was accomplished through her faith and God. Jesus was just the "cord" through which the power flowed. And, the power was able to flow through him because he was "plugged into" the Father.

So, how do we "plug into" the Father so He can use us as He used Jesus? All of creation is eagerly waiting for the manifestation of the sons of God - those who can be an *honorable representation of God* - to show themselves. How is that going to happen? How will they be recognized? Most likely in the same way Jesus was: by the acts of power and authority he performed.

As stated previously, I believe this has already begun, but only on a very small scale. Most of this manifestation has yet to take place because few Christians understand

what it means to be a son of God. It is of critical importance that true believers begin to grasp this concept of
their power and purpose as sons of God, and search out
its reality and application in their lives on this earth. This
can only manifest as we return to a deeper, individual and
personal study of the kingdom of heaven - which comes
with both *power* and *glory* (Matthew 6:13).

THE KINGDOM OF HEAVEN - KEYS & SECRETS

Jesus spoke so much about the kingdom of heaven
– 121 times by my count. Many of these references were
cloaked in the language of parables, giving the impression
that there are secrets yet to be discovered. Indeed, Jesus
spoke of the *secrets of the kingdom* when his disciples
asked for an explanation of one of his parables (Mark 4:11;
Luke 8:10). The fact that the above-mentioned manifestation of the sons of God and how it will happen is largely
yet to be revealed makes it unknown – a *secret*.

There are *keys to the kingdom* (Matthew 16:13-19).
Jesus told Peter that he gave him those keys and said they
were pivotal to the establishment of the church He came
to set up. They are also related to power and authority. A
key opens a locked door, but what lies on the other side
still has to be investigated – more *secrets*.

What are these secrets and how do we learn them?
I believe the answer to these questions will lead us to
more and greater *manifestations of the sons of God*. The
world is waiting for it! This is the topic of our next chapter.
Please join us.

CHAPTER EIGHT

THE KEYS & SECRETS OF THE KINGDOM

*"...'Who do people say the Son of Man is?'...
Peter answered, 'You are the Christ, the Son of
the living God...' Jesus answered...'no person
taught you that. My Father in heaven showed
you who I am....on this rock I will build my
church...I will give you the <u>keys of the kingdom</u>
of heaven...'"* (Matthew 16:13-19, NCV)

*"Jesus' followers asked him what this story
meant. Jesus said, 'You have been chosen to
know the <u>secrets about the kingdom</u> of God...'"*
(Luke 8:9-10, NCV)

ARRIVING AT OUR DESTINATION

We have arrived...sort of. Our journey has taken us
far with much study, definitions and pondering.
Now we find ourselves at the ultimate destination – the
kingdom of heaven. But upon our arrival we discover we

need *keys* to open it, and once opened there are *secrets* inside which need to be discerned. How much this mirrors God's infinity! Just when you think you've grasped something important about Him, you find that piece of knowledge is merely a bridge to so much more yet to be realized.

Every part of the journey is important, for growing into a mature son of God is a step-by-step process. Babies crawl before they walk, walk before they run, and they stumble along the way. So it is with us. We must grow and increase in our knowledge slowly and steadily - line upon line, precept upon precept - thinking and meditating as we do. As always, our deepest desire is for the reader to take the foundation we are laying and personally study to build your own life experiences on what you learn and discern.

ONE LAST REVIEW

Let's look over one last time where we have traveled, and see how each step equipped us with the knowledge to go to the next:

- Chapter Two – The kingdom of heaven is a present reality, not a future event. It is here now because it is *within* believers. (Luke 17:20-21)
- Chapter Three – The "end of the world" Jesus spoke of was actually the "end of an age" and not the end of planet earth. (Matthew 24)
- Chapter Four – Our greatest hope in this life is not to escape it, but to become an ever-improving and "honorable representation of God." (2 Corinthians 3:18)
- Chapter Five – We are sons of God with both inborn and *potential* character traits. Maturing and refining these character qualities increasingly

enables us to walk out our *sonship*. (Hebrews 1:3; Romans 8:29-30)

- Chapter Six – Changing our thinking – renewing our minds – is the primary battlefield in realizing and living out this *sonship*. (2 Corinthians 10:4-5)
- Chapter 7 – God has equipped us with both earthly authority (Matthew 28:18) and access to miraculous power to be able to live and rule as kings and priests in this life. (Acts 1:8; 2 Timothy 1:7)

THE KEYS TO THE KINGDOM

Let's begin with a most vital step – entrance into the kingdom of God – the place where truth, authority and power reside. Jesus told Peter that he gave him the keys to the kingdom. Why? He indicated these keys were central to the establishment of the church He came to set up. It would also seem they are very instrumental in relation to the exercise of power and authority on this earth. This passage is lengthy, but it provides so much to think about that we are going to print the majority of it, then investigate some key phrases:

> *"...he asked his followers, 'Who do people say the Son of Man is?' They answered, 'Some say you are John the Baptist. Others say you are Elijah, and still others say you are Jeremiah or one of the prophets.' Then Jesus asked them, 'And who do you say I am?' Simon Peter answered, 'You are the Christ, the Son of the living God.' Jesus answered, 'You are blessed...because no person taught you that. My Father in heaven showed you who I am.*

So, I tell you, you are Peter. On this rock <u>I will</u> <u>build my church</u> and the power of death will not be able to defeat it. I will give you the keys to the kingdom of heaven; the <u>things you don't</u> <u>allow</u> on earth will be the things that God does not allow, and the <u>things you allow on earth</u> will be the things that God allows'" (Matthew 16:15-19, NCV).

I will build my church...

Let's begin with the statement Jesus made to Peter - *On this rock I will build my church...* - and ask two questions. First, how is this *church* defined that Jesus was going to build - what kind of a church is it?

- Church – *[Greek #1577 - ekklesia - from a comp. of #1537]* an original calling out; a community of members on earth or saints in heaven or both. (<u>Strong's Concordance</u>)

This is a completely new kind of church - *an original calling out*. It is not a synagogue or temple as was the typical "church" of Jesus' day. It was to be a *community of members* – people – not a building. This was a brand new idea that Jesus was putting forth to Peter.

Second question – What is the *rock* it was to be built upon? <u>Strong's Concordance</u> reveals two distinct words for rock -

- Rock - *[Greek #4073 - petra]* – rock
- Rock – *[Greek #4074 – Petros]* – as a name, Petrus, an apostle: Peter.

This passage uses the first word – *petra* – meaning simply "rock." Jesus was not referring to building his new church of people upon Peter, but rather upon a *rock solid foundation.* Foundation of what? Letting scripture interpret scripture, let's look at the conversation just preceding this declaration for the answer.

Jesus had just asked the disciples – *Who do people say the Son of Man is?* – and they gave several answers, all of them wrong. Jesus then asked Peter the same question and his reply was – *You are the Christ, the Son of the living God.* Jesus told Peter this was not just the right answer, but added that Peter did not receive this knowledge from any man. Indeed, he said it was <u>a revelation straight from the Father in heaven!</u>

Jesus then declared <u>this</u> to be the *rock,* the foundation on which he would build his *church* - <u>a community of believers who could hear directly from God as Peter had</u>. Peter was the example and first member of this *original calling out* – an entirely new type of church: people, not a building, who could learn from God Himself and not have to depend on priests for revealing God's truth. I believe this is one of the secrets of the kingdom: The *church* Jesus desires to build is to be made up of mature sons of God who can hear directly from the Father for new revelation and daily guidance. What a concept!

Mark 1:27 records the people's reaction to much of what Jesus taught. They were continually amazed because he taught something *new.* Jesus came to create a new world, one in which the spiritual and physical worked in unity. He showed his followers how this *new world* operated in the way he lived his life: He was in constant communication with his Father. He declared openly and often that he and the Father were one, and prayed that his followers could achieve the same thing (John 17:11). This was a unity - a oneness - of heart and mind. Jesus received revelation straight from his Father in heaven, just what he declared to Peter was the foundation for the new church he came to establish.

Because of these direct revelations from God, Jesus worked in complete concert with his Father – *"... 'I tell you the truth, the Son can do nothing alone. The Son does only what he <u>sees</u> the Father doing, because the Son does whatever the Father does. The Father loves the Son and <u>shows</u> the Son all the things he himself does'"* (John 5:19-20, NCV).

How did Jesus *see* what the Father was doing? How did the Father *show* Jesus these things? These are secrets of the kingdom that can only be discovered by *individual, personal revelation* from God directly to his sons, just like Peter's revelation of the true identity of Jesus. You do not enter the kingdom of heaven by accident. It must be an intentional quest, seeking the heart and mind of God for deeper knowledge – a clear and certain perception of truth.

Next, Jesus declared that he would give the *keys to the kingdom* to Peter as a result of his being able to hear directly from God. By doing so, Jesus made Peter the founding and first member of this new church. Then Jesus makes an absolutely astounding statement of how this new church of the sons of God would operate: *The <u>things you don't allow</u> on earth will be the things that God does not allow, and the <u>things you allow on earth</u> will be the things that God allows.*

Things Allowed and Disallowed by Who?!?

This declaration has to be one of the most astonishing things Jesus ever said in all his ministry. For we know that God is sovereign over all things. We have also learned that He gave His Son *all things* along with the responsibility, power and authority to rule over or govern them. Along those same lines, we have come to understand that the *sons of God* possess this same inheritance because they are joint-heirs with Christ.

This statement from Jesus not only confirms this inheritance of ruling authority, but surely must have rendered Peter speechless as he declared the scope of the power and responsibility that God was giving over to this new church - that *He* will not interfere with *their* decisions: *the things you don't allow on earth will be the things that God does not allow, and the things you allow on earth will be the things that God allows.*

Why would He do that? God knew that this new church would be made up of fallible human beings. Sons of God are not perfect. They are learning how to rule. They are *becoming an honorable representation of the Father.* They will make right choices of what to allow and disallow as they hear directly from God and obey. But there will also be times when they step out on their own, not hearing from or obeying God, and will make horrible choices as a result, allowing some things that God would never tolerate; i.e. abortion. Yet, according to this passage, God would allow this and not overrule those poor or even tragic choices. We have to ask again, why would He do that? Perhaps, because we need to be like Jesus and learn obedience by what we suffer (Hebrews 5:8). Unlike Jesus, however, our suffering would be the consequences of the wrong choices we make.

Jesus prayed that the Father's will be *done on earth as it is in heaven* (Matthew 6:10). Yet, based on the previous statement, He will not force this to happen. He is depending on His sons to bring it to pass. Incredible. How do we bring this prayer to fruition? It will require personal and group effort. How do the sons of God find one another and unite – become one with each other as Jesus prayed in John 17:11? I believe it will occur as we use both the keys to the kingdom and the subsequent discerning of the secrets of the kingdom.

The keys will open the door to the possibilities. To learn the possibilities - the secrets - you must step through that door and start searching for answers. I humbly share with you my thoughts on what I believe to be two keys necessary to enter the kingdom. (There are many more, to be sure.)

<u>YOUR THOUGHTS - ONE KEY TO THE KINGDOM</u>

The kingdom message is about who you are and how you fit in the kingdom of heaven. As you find your place in God's kingdom, you will find your life. Most people's frustration lies in their belief that they are not doing anything important with their lives. To overcome this belief, we must renew our minds.

To renew your mind you must put something new into it. How about this: You are important! You were created as a totally unique individual, in the image of God Himself. You were created to be an overcomer (John 16:33). This means there is something to overcome. This process begins in your mind. Some of life's circumstances and some of the people in our lives who come against us are our "trainers." They are not the problem. It is what we *think* about them that can be the problem. Can you take your peace in the midst of the storm or do you allow others to ruin your day...your life?

We need to ask ourselves, "What is it that drives me every day?" When we come into this world, God has equipped us with everything we need to overcome. Is what you believe helping you overcome, or are you being overcome because of what you believe? Your life can only manifest what you believe. Right thinking gives us the ability to do what we could not do before. Henry Ford said, "If you think you can or you think you can't, you're right."

Muslims and non-believers are changing the world because of what they think - what they believe. Their actions are not prophecy in motion. They are darkness trying to take over the light. As sons of God and citizens of the kingdom of heaven, we have the assignment - the purpose and power - to overcome this darkness. Unfortunately, we have been taught to listen and obey the voice of the world for so long that we have failed to engage our communities. We are not speaking up in the face of lies, error and even crime (violating the Constitution, the laws of nature and nature's God).

Our minds - our thoughts - are the only thing that stop us from being what we are supposed to be, being who God says we are: priests and kings! We are not in this world to conform to it. We are here to transform it. This is the purpose of the sons of God. As we take our thoughts captive to believe God, He will give us the eyes to see the possibilities in life, not just the obstacles. (Romans 12:2)

As we do this, we find another key to the kingdom.

EMULATING JESUS - ANOTHER KEY TO THE KINGDOM

The birth of Christ was the first time in history that God put Himself *into* a human being: a man was born with

God in him! Jesus came to this world and died so that we might have access to a place no man had before: The way to the Father is through Jesus. But he also came to show us how to live in this world. God should be able to reveal Himself *through* us, not just *to* us. God *in* you is what the gospel is about.

John the Baptist preached repentance as the foundation for a new life. Jesus said, "Follow me," and then taught about living that new life in the kingdom of heaven. The foundation is necessary, but we do not live in a foundation. We build on it. If all we focus on is repenting and man's "sin nature" we are missing the true gospel message. That "sin nature" has been rectified through the sacrificial death and resurrection of Jesus. We should be showing the "God nature" more than the "sinful nature." Our true spiritual nature is to become more like God and less like ourselves (going from glory to glory).

We must go beyond the message of a baby in the manger and Jesus on the cross, and grow into a son of God in the kingdom. We must learn what it means to have Jesus in us, and learn to get ready to be "one with the Father" as Jesus was. We talk about what Jesus did. We should also be talking about what Jesus wants to do *in* us and *through* us. Jesus taught more about the kingdom of heaven than any other subject. This should be our focus as well.

We have much to learn, and a tremendous need to grow in our relationship with and knowledge of our heavenly Father. So how do we go about becoming one with the Father as Jesus did? How do we align our thoughts with God's thoughts? Answers to these questions must truly be more of the secrets of the kingdom. Let's see what scripture says about these secrets.

THE SECRETS OF THE KINGDOM

Why did Jesus frame so much of what he taught in parables? The kingdom of heaven is like a man who sowed good seed...a grain of mustard seed...leaven that a woman took and hid...hidden treasure...a merchant in search of fine pearls...a net. (Matthew 13:24, 31, 33, 44, 45, 47) Why did he not clearly speak out his message? The kingdom is.... and then make a unambiguous declaration. Why did he so often answer a question with a question? Why was the message of the kingdom so cloaked in *secrets*?

One such story is found in the book of Luke, where Jesus was teaching a very large crowd of people. He told them the parable of the farmer sowing seed and the various outcomes of that planting. At the end of the story there are two separate and fascinating exchanges – Jesus first addressing the entire crowd, and then turning his attention to his followers:

> "*...As Jesus finished the story, he called out, 'You people who can hear me, listen!' Jesus' followers asked him what this story meant. Jesus said, 'You have been <u>chosen</u> to know the <u>secrets</u> about the kingdom of God. But I use stories to speak to other people so that: 'They will look, but they may not see. They will listen, but they may not understand'*" (Luke 8:8-10, NCV).

What did Jesus mean – *you have been chosen to know the secrets* – but others cannot? Why? Doesn't he want everyone to know these secrets?

OUR OWN PARABLE – WHO WILL DISCOVER THE SECRETS?

As we study and our eyes begin to open we will see, speak and understand things we could not previously. 1 Corinthians 4:1-5 makes it clear that God is still revealing things, but only certain people are trusted with these secrets. The secrets of the kingdom are for those who are saved, but more specifically for the sons of God – those who want more than salvation.

The majority of these secrets of the kingdom are not written down. They are discerned through meditation. We have to dig them out. We must ask. We must seek. We must desire more. *"God is honored for what he keeps secret. Kings are honored for what they can discover"* (Proverbs 25:2, NCV). The secrets of the kingdom are to make us better, stronger, gain more knowledge of how the world works, improve relationships, have better health, learn how to help others change their attitudes. We have access to these secrets, but we must *discover* them.

If Jesus had plainly spoken out the secrets, they would no longer be secrets. In addition, if these secrets are taught from the pulpit, they will not be valued as highly as if we had to search for them on our own. Jesus bluntly referred to giving away these precious secrets to the crowds as *casting pearls before swine* (Matthew 7:6). Secrets of the kingdom are precious and to be highly valued, not revealed indiscriminately. The principle is one of working to own something as opposed to having it given to you. Let's look at a modern day parable of the Jones, Brown and Smith families:

The entire Jones family does not like to work, so they are on government assistance - welfare. They receive monthly checks, money they did not work to earn. This money is usually poorly managed and they often complain they need more, but they expect the "more" to come from others, and don't even think about getting a job. They not only contribute nothing to the community, they put a drain on it. They live out their lives as helpless victims, always in need, never learning any of the secrets of prosperity.

The Brown family are all gainfully employed, working for a local company, Smith's Innovations. The Browns are very careful with their money because they earned it. They have a budget, stick to it, have a nice house and two cars. They contribute to their community both through their work - what they produce - and the purchases they make. They know and have applied some of the secrets of prosperity.

The Smith family are the neighborhood entrepreneurs. They studied hard, took a few calculated risks and started Smith's Innovations which employs a few dozen employees. They live in a large, very nice house with a three-car garage, and hire a housecleaner and groundskeeper to help with the upkeep. They contribute the most to their communities, including providing jobs for others who will, in turn, help the neighborhood. As self-starters, they choose to continue to study and learn, and find more ways to serve the needs of those around them and make more money. Their only limits are the ones they choose; i.e. how many hours to work, how many clients and employees they want, how much to produce, etc. They know even more of the secrets of prosperity than the Brown family and spread some of this knowledge to others.

What *secret of the kingdom* is hidden in these three scenarios?

The Jones family represents people who depend completely on others to teach them. They have a welfare mentality. They go to church every Sunday and listen to what the pastor teaches. But they don't truly learn or apply much of what they hear because the knowledge isn't <u>theirs</u>. There was no cost to it, no investment of themselves, of their reading time or meditative thoughts. They will discover none of the *secrets of the kingdom.*

The Brown family is like those who study the Bible in a small group format. They discover more truth and will probably apply more of it since they have looked deeper into the Word for themselves. But since this study is directed by others, their results will still be limited because their personal thoughts and questions were not necessarily addressed, but rather, those of the group. These people will learn some of the *secrets of the kingdom,* but not enough to bring cultural transformation.

The Smith family are the ones we want to emulate. These are the people who will discover the most *secrets of the kingdom* - the self-starters, the sons of God who privately <u>choose</u> to study and ask their own questions as the Spirit of God leads them. This is the most powerful teaching of all because God alone knows their mind and heart, what they know and what they need to know. This individualized teaching, one-on-one from the God of the universe, will reveal the *secrets of the kingdom* and those who hear will be transformed personally and will begin to transform their world as well.

Likewise, as Jesus individually taught the followers who came and asked more questions after the parables, it is evident that the ones *chosen* to know the secrets of the kingdom have themselves *chosen* to seek out these secrets. It is not Jesus who withholds them. It is the sons of God who search them out, and will, therefore, find them.

EXAMPLES OF THE SECRETS

The secrets of the kingdom are both concealed and revealed. Some of the secrets that God shares with us are for our personal edification and correction, and not to be shared. Other secrets involve God revealing spiritual truths. Still more uncover scientific or natural laws of the universe. These secrets are given for the benefit of all mankind. The discovery and subsequent use of these secrets of the kingdom are as varied as the people and the gifts God has given them. Our God-created universe is full of such secrets.

Isaac Newton uncovered the secrets of gravity, motion and mathematics that led to many innovations and improvements in our lives. George Washington Carver, who called God his "lab partner," unlocked countless secrets of peanuts and sweet potatoes, and brought economic prosperity to the South as a result. Cyrus McCormick advanced civilization and destroyed famine in America by inventing a reaper. Joseph Lister was the founder of antiseptic surgery, saving incalculable lives as a result.

Each of these men was a true son of God as they not only discovered secrets of the kingdom, but blessed mankind with them. They all started from a foundation of faith, studied in whatever area of gifting God had given them, and then built upon it. *"...stir up the gift of God which is in you..."* (2 Timothy 1:6). George Washington Carver studied for years in a laboratory, experimenting and breaking down the various constituencies of sweet potatoes and peanuts. Had he not done so, he would not have been able to understand what God showed him, which ultimately led to more than 400 products he created from just one vegetable and one legume!

The discoveries of these men became the foundation for others who followed them to build upon with even more breakthroughs. Every one of these uncovered secrets, used properly, can be an advancement of the kingdom of God. God gives every one of us a gift. It can be worked out spiritually and physically. Do you know your gift? Are you stirring it up? What is it you love to do? What are your "hot buttons" in life? Study more, get involved and see what God will show you.

These are just a few examples of the secrets of the kingdom – some from God's scientific, natural laws of the physical universe, and others are spiritual secrets wrapped in parables or waiting to be discovered through a deeper study of the Word. How do you find the secrets God wants to reveal to you? God doesn't scream His secrets from the rafters. He whispers them into your heart. I'd like to share my thoughts about how some of these may be discovered, and hopefully inspire you to begin your own search.

LEARNING THE SECRETS OF THE KINGDOM

As Christians, our new life begins when we are saved, born again. If we stop there, simply waiting to go to heaven, we will miss the purpose and fulfillment for which God created us. God has equipped every one of his children with the capacity to mature into sons of God who can learn to discern some of these secrets of the kingdom. How do we do that? Not just by reading God's Word, but by studying it, meditating upon it.

The method of study that has been demonstrated throughout these booklets is one way to discern some of these secrets. We'll set it forth one more time as we go deeply into a scripture I believe to be one of the keys to the secrets of the kingdom - *"For God has not given us the spirit of fear, but of power and of love and of a sound mind"* (2 Timothy 1:7, NKJV).

We begin by defining some terms, and then reasoning through their meaning in regard to what we want to learn –

- Spirit – *the rational <u>soul</u>; vital principle, mental disposition* (<u>Strong's Concordance</u>)
- Soul – *that part of a man which enables him to think and reason and renders him a subject of moral government; internal, active power* (<u>Webster's 1828</u>)
- Fear – *timidity; [from #1169] dread; faithless* (<u>Strong's Concordance</u>)
- Timidity – *want of courage or boldness to face danger; habitual cowardice* (<u>Webster's 1828</u>)

Briefly re-stated, God has not given us the *mental disposition* – the thought, idea or way of thinking – to be cowardly, lacking in courage or boldness to fear <u>anything</u>! He has not supplied us with a *want of courage* to face danger. What He has provided is a spirit of power, love and a sound mind.

- Power - *[Greek – dunamis] – miraculous power, strength, mighty work* (<u>Strong's Concordance</u>)
- Love – *[Greek #25 – agape] – affection or benevolence; charity* (<u>Strong's Concordance</u>)
- Love – *[Greek #5360 – philadelphia or phileo] – brotherly love* (<u>Strong's Concordance</u>)

We already discussed the incredible miraculous *dunamis power* in Volume 6, power that comes straight from God and passes through us to assist others. The *love* given to us in this passage is *agape.* I have added the second definition to better understand the first.

Phileo love is brotherly love, a kindly, affectionate feeling. While this is a wonderful emotion, it is just that: a *feeling* that comes and goes with circumstances. *Agape* love is a mental, deliberate, charitable choice that has nothing to do with emotions. It is a conscious assent of the will as a matter of principle or duty. It is the love that loves the unlovable. Only God can demonstrate this kind of unde-served love on a consistent basis. This is the *spirit of love* that God gives us, thus equipping us with this love and empowering us to execute it with miraculous, *dunamis power* to care for those the world casts aside (including those who often present the greatest challenge: yourself and your family).

Lastly, He has given us the spirit of a *sound mind.* This is one word in Greek, from <u>Strong's Concordance</u>, and to build greater understanding we are following it with a series of augmenting definitions from <u>Webster's 1828</u> -

- Sound mind – *[Greek #4995 –sophronismos]* <u>*disci-*</u> <u>*pline*</u>*; self-control* (<u>Strong's Concordance</u>)
- Sound [mind #13] – *sound understanding or reason; perfect intellect; not broken or defective; not enfee-bled by age or accident; not wild or wandering; not <u>deranged</u>: Founded in truth; firm; strong; valid; cannot be overthrown or refuted. Right; free from error; <u>orthodox</u>*
- Orthodox – *sound in the Christian faith; believing the genuine doctrines taught in the scriptures.*

- Discipline – *to instruct and govern; to teach rules and practice, and accustom to order and subordination.*
- Deranged – *put out of order; disturbed; embarrassed; confused; disordered in mind; delirious or distracted.*
- Subordination – *the state of being under control or government*

This is a very, very long list of definitions, but I've included them to supply the reader with lots of personal meditation material. I urge you to think long and hard on the scope of this *sound mind,* and the fact that it belongs to you as a son of God. It is a gift from your Heavenly Father. Below are just *some* of the applications to consider:

God has given His sons the ability to think and reason through their daily situations. We do not have to simply react to people and circumstances, but can actually mull over what our responses should be. But we will need to do it on purpose. It won't happen naturally.

Our world today is so cluttered with noise and distractions. We wake up to a clock radio and end our day in front of the television. In between we are bombarded with cell phones, computers and Ipods. All this audio/visual stimuli blocks our ability to think and reason through the things that matter most. God speaks to us in a still, small voice. He doesn't shout over sound bytes and video images.

A personal example: I listen to USA Radio News when I wake up. It gives over 15 stories in less than five minutes - about 20 seconds per story. This data dump of information, with no time to think through any of it, plants fear (or wild, wandering thoughts) in my brain, for news stories are generally <u>bad news</u>. In five short minutes, 15 fearful thoughts have been introduced to my mind with no time to reason through any of them to discern what I need to do, or if I even need to be concerned, or even know about it at all. One 20-second story after another assails my brain with no opportunity to think, reason, pray for or dismiss the preceding 20 second story.

By the end of the broadcast, I can't even recall what half the stories were, yet the fearful or wandering thoughts entered my mind. There was no opportunity to exercise control over the fear because there was no quiet time to allow my spirit (rational soul) to turn my mind from turmoil to peace. Agitation and stress begins. Is there anything in your life that ushers in this kind of mental chaos?

Let's examine another aspect of this verse. One of the definitions of spirit is *mental disposition.* One of the duties of your soul is not just to *think and reason,* but to render yourself subject to moral government. In other words, the purpose of your soul's thinking and reasoning is to bring you to the place of making right decisions and performing right actions. *Right* actions are according to the will of God. Going through this soul process – thinking and reasoning, then doing what is right – will lead to the proper mental disposition of your spirit.

Your spirit must be trained to do what is right. What does the spirit in you do? What is it you are training it for? Thinking? Hearing God? A spirit is not flesh that can accomplish physical work. Your spirit is your intangible inner man. It is the inner man that drives the outer man – your flesh – into action. This makes that training of the spirit to think right thoughts of tremendous importance, for this will determine your emotional and physical health, the quality of your relationships, and what you do every day.

Therefore, circumventing our ability to think through the events we hear about or are currently doing, circumvents the proper care and development of our spirits. It greatly hinders our ability to hear God speak to us. God has not given us the spirit of fear, but it is this spirit that pervades and prevails when we have a steady "diet" of a hurried and harried life style – television, radio, telephone, texting – <u>constant noise</u>!

God has given us the spirit of power, love and a sound mind, but these spirits are set in motion only when we have taken the *quiet time* to think about and study them. They do not enter your spirit in quick sound bytes. They only enter through quiet, intentional study and meditation. They do not enter simply because you know about them and read of their existence – in other words, reading about them in scripture. Bible reading gives you knowledge of their existence. But knowledge alone (*a clear and certain perception of truth*) is not enough!

Scripture says in James 2:19 (my paraphrase) – *You believe in God? Big deal! So do the demons and even they have enough sense to tremble with that knowledge. What does your knowledge of God make you do?*

Knowledge alone is almost worse than useless. For having the knowledge makes you accountable. You cannot claim innocence through ignorance. What we must have to properly train our spirit into right thinking is –

- Wisdom – *right use of knowledge* (<u>Webster's 1828</u>)

Let's relate what we've learned: God has given you the spirit of power, love and a sound mind. What does that mean to you in regard to learning the secrets of the kingdom? How does that help you train your spirit to think right? How do you turn this knowledge into useful power for right thinking, overpowering the spirit of fear that bombards you every moment of every busy, over-filled day?

By stepping out of the busy day and deliberately setting aside some quiet time to reflect and meditate, listen, write out and personalize this scripture (and others). Turn off the television. Shut off your cell phone. Study, learn, write down in a journal what the spirit of power is – the definition and some personal applications. Then ask God to keep that revelation and new thought in the front of your mind throughout the rest of the day.

Think you don't have time? God says this personal study time is your first priority: *"Seek first the kingdom of God and His righteousness and all these things shall be added to you"* (Matthew 6:13, NKJV). See to the things of God's kingdom *first* (remembering the kingdom is *inside* you...your thoughts), and all else will fall into the proper place. The fact is you cannot afford to *not* seek these truths. Big changes are upon us in this world and the only way we will be properly equipped is through learning the secrets of the kingdom.

USE YOUR NEW SECRET

After you have found a new truth - a secret of the kingdom - bring it with you into the front of your thoughts throughout the day. This takes discipline and practice. Choose to make your new revelation that God gave you in your quiet time the *sieve* that every other thought must pass through. When you practice this discipline you are retraining your soul - your mind - to not only think and reason, but to choose an action based on the supremacy of God's spirit of power, love and a sound mind *over* the spirit of fear.

For some of us, just meditating on some of the phrases within the definition of *sound mind - perfect intellect; not broken or defective; not enfeebled by age or accident; not wild or wandering; not deranged* - will begin our mental and spiritual transformation. God gave this mind to you. It is a gift. Receive it. This in turn, will cause you to make right decisions, to do right things and begin training your spirit in the right mental disposition or thoughts.

This will not happen by chance. This will not happen because you know you have access to this spirit of power, love and a sound mind. This will only happen when you take time, when you get away from the noise of the world, when you get out not just your Bible, but study guides (i.e. Concordance and dictionaries as we've done in these booklets), and personal journal. Read. Study. Listen. Write. Believe. Receive. Here's a great verse to spur you forward – "...*the kingdom of heaven suffers violence and the violent take it by force*" (Matthew 11:12, NKJV). My study of these words makes this translate to – The kingdom of heaven is being seized by the energetic, who take it by force.

Make this your new goal – be energetic and forceful in your meditations! Keep your fresh revelation in the *front* of your mind every day. Freedom from fear and wrong thoughts will begin. God will continue to show you more of the secrets of the kingdom. Process and re-process, think and re-think this new thought from God. This points to the absolute necessity of a journal, for it enables you to go back and feed your spirit again and again on the specific revelation or message God gave you, by reading your journal entries over and over again.

Re-reading these entries not only refreshes your spirit and reminds your mind, but the meditation time spent there can deepen that revelation and allow God to take you to the next layer or level of understanding. Write it down as well. The first word was the seed. The development of the thought is the plant that will spring up and ultimately bring forth fruit or positive change in your mind, which will heal your heart and change your life. You'll be walking daily in the kingdom of God.

GOD'S PROMISES ABOUT HIS SECRETS

Discovering the secrets of the kingdom is what God wants you to do.

- *"...He is a rewarder of them that diligently seek him"* (Hebrews 11:6, NKJV). That's a promise!
- *"The secret things belong to the Lord our God, but those things which are revealed belong to us and to our children forever..."* (Deuteronomy 29:29, NKJV). He wants us to discover His secrets and when we do our children benefit as well.
- *"The Lord tells his secrets to those who respect him... "*(Psalm 25:14 NCV). Another wonderful promise!
- *"Before the Lord God does anything, he tells his plans to his servants the prophets"* (Amos 3:7, NCV). Are you listening?

UNVEILING THE END TIMES – DISCOVERING THE NEW HOPE!

Throughout history there have been endings, and they have all been followed by new and better beginnings. History is not linear; it is cyclical. The flood in Noah's day looked like the end of the world, but the reality was a fresh start for God's remnant. When Christ died on the cross it looked like the end of all hope, the greatest tragedy the world had ever witnessed. In fact, it was the end...of the Old Covenant. His resurrection ushered in the beginning of the New Covenant which was not only far superior to the old, but included the possibility of a new, intimate relationship between God and man that had never existed before.

We chose to re-title this book, "The POWER of Hope" with the certain belief that the New Covenant brings believers – the sons of God – to a new beginning, a greater measure of the kingdom of heaven manifested on earth, just as Jesus prayed so long ago. This includes the capacity Jesus also spoke of – being one with the Father. While this is indeed "good news" it also carries the pains of change.

End times are tough times. So are new beginnings. Though Christ started the New Covenant at the moment of his resurrection, nearly forty years passed before the Old Covenant was finally wiped out with the destruction of Jerusalem and the temple in 70 A.D. Those "end times" were exceedingly difficult, filled with combinations of both battles and death, victory and blessings.

We face monumental trials in the days to come. But God never abandons His children (Hebrews 13:5). He does not promise to remove us from the battles, but He does declare our victory in them when He says that we are more than conquerers (Romans 8:37). He does not promise us a world without tribulation but says Jesus has overcome it (John 16:33) and so can we! He even says we can have peace in the midst of these trials and trib- ulations. Throughout these chapters we have presented many, many scriptures for the reader to meditate upon to find truth, strength and direction.

As a son of God you were born to make manifest the glory of God that is within you. Most of all, we must seize the opportunity to mature as sons of God, growing in our relationship and ability to hear from the Father, seeking to become one with Him just as Jesus was. We are to be members of the new church Jesus established – individuals who can receive direct revelation from God.

The message of Jesus was simple: change your heart; change your mind; find a new way to think. America, indeed the entire world, needs something that will make us rethink what we have done to ourselves. We need to get our eyes and hearts off of what God may someday do, and instead grasp more fully what He *is* doing now and wants us to do *today*. The kingdom message will open your mind to many possibilities. We are to build something better for our posterity. If we change our minds we will change the world.

Our job is to conquer, not by violence, but by truth. No one can stop truth. It will come forth. Will you be the one to bring it? Sons of God are radical participants in a high- commitment endeavor. This is why the keys to the kingdom and the secrets of the kingdom are for them. We must find them, learn them and use them in the coming days.

CHAPTER NINE

EPILOGUE
ANOTHER PERSONAL LETTER
TO THE READER –
USING THE KEYS AND SECRETS!

Dear Reader,

We began this book with a personal letter and we end it in the same way. Our opening letter was to encourage you to study for yourself to find truth and revelation. Our closing letter is to embolden you to *use* what you have discovered.

God's word declares you to be a *royal priest* (1 Peter 2:9). Royalty is a king, one who rules the earthly world. A priest is one who sees to the things of God. Both titles belong to you as a son of God. Jesus prayed for God's kingdom to come and that His will be done on *earth* as it is in heaven – a job uniquely fitting a royal priest.

A friend and evangelist, Randy Newberry, who has since gone on to be with the Lord, gave a message a few years ago about kings, keys and secrets of the kingdom.

It deeply impacted me and I'd like to share some of his words as a final encouragement and marching orders for each of us:

"Kings don't settle for the obvious. They don't settle for the way things look. They search out a matter. They look deeper. They meditate longer. They pray harder. They want answers. They know the decisions they make affect other people and they want to make the right decisions.

"Kings don't sit and wait for things to happen. Kings make things happen. Kings are go-getters. Kings plan while others play. They stay one step ahead. The devil doesn't worry them. They worry the devil.

"Kings are passionate while others are pacified. It's something they have to do. It's a drive in their heart. They aren't reading history. They're making history. Kings don't settle for mere entertainment. Kings persist when everyone else quits. They don't know the meaning of giving up. I don't know about you, but I want to be a king. I am a king. God called me to this. God placed this in my heart. I didn't plan on it. I didn't ask for it. God has called you too. Do it with all your heart.

"God has said, '*I'm calling kings and priests all over the world. If you will rise up you can let that spirit that is within you begin to rise up and take you places, realize who you are, and stand up.*' Look in the mirror and say, I am a king and I am a priest in the kingdom of God and I have been called for such a time as this. I'm going to make decrees. I'm going to take my place and no one is going to take my place. I'm going to do what God called me to do. I'm going to finish my course. Are you ready to take this on?

"God doesn't want to save you over and over again. He wants to you realize that you are saved and that you are kings and priests in this world and you have a job to do.

Get on with the business. Uncover the secrets. Let them be revealed. God brought us to the kingdom for such a time as this. He is revealing His secrets through us. He said, *"I have given you this treasure in earthen vessels."* Christ in you is the mystery that has been hidden through all ages and is now being revealed. This also means the secrets you need to fulfill your call are hidden in the people around you. Look better at the people around you: people praying for you, supporting you, teaching you. They are the people God is using to make you who He has called you to be.

God says, *"I am your power, your strength. I will do it through you."* You don't have to see how it's going to work. He needs obedience. The kingdom of God is going to be run by God. It is being set up on this earth, but it is going to be God who runs it, through those people who will hear and obey. It's not about you. It's about God revealing himself through you. He is the secret. Serve like Jesus. God wants to reveal His secret, and the secret is you, the Christ in you, the ability that He has placed within you. This is what God is bringing to the forefront and this is what the kingdom is based upon. It's Him moving. It's Him speaking.

"Get better with the gifts. Mature. Grow up. Get past getting mad at people. Get past your ego. The kingdom is about Him. It's not about us, but He is going to use us. We get to be involved in it. Signs and wonders liberate us from the tyranny of the impossible. They are not the point. They point to the point.

"This thing that God is doing in each of us is much bigger than we can know. What God is doing in this hour is bigger than all of us. It will take all of us working together to get it accomplished. God declares, *'I have called you into the kingdom for this and I'm raising you up.'* He wants to show off His glory through us. Get ready."

Amen. This is the POWER of Hope.

ENDNOTES

1   Whiston, William, ed. and trans., The Works of Josephus, The Wars of the Jews. Peabody, Mass: Hendrickson Publishers, 1992, page 741.

2   Ibid, page 750

3   Ibid, page 741.

4   Ibid, page 737.

5   Seneca, Lucius Annaeus, ca. 4 BC-65 AD (e), Lucilium Epistulae Morales, www.archive.org n.p. Web. 2 Feb. 2010, http://www.archive.org/details/adluciliumepistu03seneuoft

6   Maier, Paul L., ed. and trans., Eusebius – The Church History. Grand Rapids: Kregel Publications, 1999, pages 100-101.

7   Clement of Alexandria, ca. 182-202 AD (e), Book One -The Stromata, www.earlychristianwritings,com n.p. Web. 2 Feb. 2010, http://www.earlychristianwritings.com/text/clement-stromata-book1.html

8   John Assaraf, The Answer: Grow Any Business, Achieve Financial Freedom, and Live an Extraordinary Life (New York: Atria Paperback, 2008) p.70

CPSIA information can be obtained
at www.ICGtesting.com
Printed in the USA
LVHW111340190821
695597LV00004B/49